THE RIGHT TO WORK

THE RIGHT
TO WORK

THE STORY OF THE
UPPER CLYDE
CONFRONTATION

Alasdair Buchan

With an introduction by the
Rt. Hon. Harold Wilson, O.B.E., M.P.

PHOTOGRAPHS BY
ARTHUR FOSTER & GEORGE WILKIE

Calder and Boyars

First published in Great Britain in 1972
by Calder & Boyars Ltd
18 Brewer Street London W1

ISBN 0 7145 0934 5 Cloth Edition
ISBN 0 7145 0935 3 Paper Edition

Printed in Great Britain by
Latimer Trend & Co Ltd
Whitstable, Kent

CONTENTS

ACKNOWLEDGEMENTS

The author would like to thank:

Harold Wilson for agreeing to write the Introduction

The library staffs of the Glasgow Herald and Daily Record.

John Calder of the Daily Record for suggesting the first paragraph of Chapter XI.

Douglas Malone, Andrew Hargrave and Jack McGill for various help and advice.

Mrs. Rosemary Baillie and Miss Norma Dewar for secretarial help.

Lewis Chester and Professor Ken Alexander for reading the manuscript.

Mr. Martin Wright for the back cover photograph.

Above all the shop stewards of U.C.S. for everything.

To the late William Hutchison

INTRODUCTION

The story of the Upper Clyde in 1971 - a story which, at the moment of writing, has not ended - is the story of a community which was not prepared to lie down in defeat, victim of a dogma rooted in the nineteenth century. Clydebank was not willing to submit itself to a crude butchery dressed up as painless surgery from a Government determined to impose a doctrinaire solution, regardless of economics or social humanity.

But for the men who work on the Upper Clyde, this story would have followed its conventional course: meetings between management and men would have resulted in failure to agree; the inevitable sackings would have been accompanied by forlorn protest; the dole would have been started and the story would have ended. Ended, that is, except for Clydebank and the families who lived there; families whose predecessors made Clydeside the cradle of the world's shipbuilding industry would have followed its hearse to the grave-yard of unwanted skills.

That that did not happen - that this book is entitled The Right to Work rather than The Town That Was Murdered - is a tribute to Clydesiders who were not willing to sit back and respond as convention dictated. They declared that no man, no Minister, no Government had the right recklessly or through ignorance and prejudice to jeopardise their lives or the lives of their families. Whether it was the right reaction quickly became irrelevant: it was a natural reaction to an obsolete ideology. What the men of the Clyde proclaimed, and what I went to Clydeside to assert, was 'the right to work'. And that principle cannot, and must not, be denied.

Harold Wilson
December 1971

FOREWORD

The two young girls from Interflora came in
carrying a large bunch of red roses and giggling.
They took the flowers up to the chairman who read
the card to the forty members of the Joint Shop
Stewards Co-ordinating Committee. It said: 'To the
workers of U.C.S. Good luck - from John and Yoko.'
A steward asked: 'But are you sure it's from them?'
'Well,' said the indignant chairman, 'do you know any
other John and Yoko?'. 'No,' shouted a steward
happily, 'but we know another Lenin.'

It was the end of the first week of the famous
'work-in' at Upper Clyde Shipbuilders Ltd. The men
at the meeting were at the centre of the greatest
industrial struggle in Britain for many decades.
They were the leaders of a workforce of 8,500 men
who had been told that they were no longer required,
but who had turned round and said: 'No. We have a
right to work and we will work.' They had taken over
control of the four divisions of the U.C.S. consortium
and now claimed to be running them.

Their action, and the public campaign which
sprang up around it, involved much more than a
redundancy fight. It stemmed from a reaction to the
rundown of industry and employment in Clydeside
and Scotland. The stewards were not only battling
against the liquidator who was now in charge. They
had taken up arms against the Government and its
policies.

And they were receiving backing, to an extent
never before given to an unofficial action, from every
section of the Labour movement, from nearly every

political party, and from many broader based sections of the community.

Indeed, a whole town of 50, 000 people practically put its entire services, from the municipal bank to the dust carts, at the disposal of the shop stewards.

Why were a group of joiners, painters, electricians and boilermakers able to command such tremendous national and international support? After all, other British industries like mining and railways had been run down with far more men losing their jobs without the great outcry which greeted the U.C.S. redundancies.

There are several reasons - notably the emotive name of Clydebank, 'Scotland's Jarrow' of the thirties, known the world over as the town that builds ships - but most basic is the 'work-in' itself.

Many people read into the situation much more than there was, more than was intended. There was talk of workers' control, workers' communes, workers' revolution. These were exaggerations, but not great ones. The stewards had adopted a completely new form of industrial action, initiated and controlled by the workers themselves. They were inside, not outside, the gates, and they were working normally.

Unlike previous situations of mass redundancy, known only too well to the Scots, the men themselves were not willing to merely protest, march, petition or lobby, though they did these things.

They took one step more.

They asserted their right to work in the most physical way possible, by continuing to build ships after being sacked. For not only were they unwilling to accept the social depression of the long dole queue, they did not accept that the redundancies even made economic sense.

This is the story of Upper Clyde Shipbuilders, of the 'work-in' and the battle to save 8, 500 jobs, but more than anything to save the tradition of shipbuilding on the Clyde - and the proud name of 'Clyde Built'.

I

'WE HAVE TAKEN OVER THE YARDS'

At 10.30 a.m. the reporters and T.V. crews arrived
at the gates of the U.C.S. shipyard in Clydebank to
attend the mass meeting called for that morning. It
was Friday 30 July 1971, and the Government had
decided the day before that the yard along with another
should be closed.

But as they arrived at the yard entrance they were
politely told by company gateman Alex Stewart that
he had been instructed not to admit the media. A
young boilermaker's steward who had been assigned
to keep a watch on the gates ran down the cobbled
yard to the convener's office to pass on what he had
seen.

As he passed the apprentice's classroom the forty-
strong co-ordinating committee of the yards were
leaving after their meeting to discuss the impending
closures. They intended to hold a short press
conference before the mass meeting.

This was the chance they had looked for. For the
previous six weeks they had talked of a 'takeover' of
the yard. Now they had a chance to demonstrate in a
visible way that they were now in charge.

Clydebank deputy convener Gerry Ross was
dispatched to tell Stewart, who had been at the yard
barrier since it had been raised again after the six
years closure in the depression of the thirties, to
admit the press.

Ross and the gatemen's steward John McGonagall
formally told him that the yards were now being
controlled by the stewards. He would now take his
orders from them and not the liquidator, or the

Government.

The press walked down the cobbled yard to the open area next to the Fitting Out Berth where the 3,500 yard workers had gathered beneath the high gantry cranes that symbolise a Clydeside skyline.

The leading stewards went onto the platform amid scattered cheers from the men. The meeting began with the announcement that the yards had new bosses.

The full-time yard convener Bobby Dickie, a quiet-spoken Scot with militant, though non-party, views told them: 'We decided to hold a press conference after a meeting of shop stewards today but the management - or rather the liquidator - refused to allow the press and T.V. into the yards.

'As a first move to show we have taken over the yards, we let the press and T.V. in for this meeting. This is the press conference.'

The co-ordinating committee's main spokesman, engineering steward James Reid gave a report on the visit to London by the stewards to hear the announcement by the Government that the company were to lose two yards, and 6,000 men.

To cheers he said: 'This is the first campaign of its kind in trade unionism. We are not going on strike. We are not even having a sit in. We do not recognise that there should be any redundancies and we are going to "work-in".

'We are taking over the yards because we refuse to accept that faceless men can take these decisions. We are not strikers. We are responsible people and we will conduct ourselves with dignity and discipline.'

And he laid down the code of conduct for all those working in the stewards' controlled yards. 'There will be no hooliganism, there will be no vandalism, and there will be no bevvying (drinking).

'We are not the wildcats, we want to work. The real wildcats are in Number Ten, Downing Street. They are the hardest-faced bunch of political gangsters I have ever met. They make Al Capone and his gunmen look like a troop of Boy Scouts.

'The biggest mistake we could make is to lie down, capitulate and grovel to them.'

14

He ended his tough speech with the traditional Clydebank boast, 'We don't only build ships on the Clyde, we build men. They have taken on the wrong people and we will fight. '

The morning's events came at the end of a six-week hiatus in the life of Upper Clyde Shipbuilders Ltd. In mid-June the company had been put into liquidation after the Conservative Government had declined to give a further £6 million to the company to ease a shortage of working capital.

Six weeks later the Secretary of State for Trade and Industry, John Davies had announced that the company was only going to have the Govan yard and the Linthouse steel fabrication division as its base.

The other two yards, Clydebank and Scotstoun, and most of the labour force were to go.

Now the stewards had taken action. At lunchtime they placed Clydebank steward John McComish, who had worked on the Queen Elizabeth and Queen Mary before the war, in charge of security for the whole company. A twenty-four-hour rota for manning the gates was drawn up. The stewards - there were over 200 in the company - were given instructions that they should stop all traffic coming in or going out in order to watch for signs of a rundown of capital equipment. In particular any scrapmen arriving at the gate, normally for industrial waste, were to be questioned closely.

That afternoon the committee went to see the liquidator, Robert Courtney Smith, to tell him he was no longer in control. He had announced at a press conference in Glasgow in the morning that he intended to begin phasing out the labour force almost immediately.

He had said that between 200 and 400 workers, mainly staff, would be paid off in August. After them more than 1, 000 men from all divisions would be paid off on a phased programme up to the beginning of October. Further lay-offs would depend on the progress on ships already under way.

For over an hour the stewards argued their case with Mr. Smith, with the discussion tending to one side as the men told him what he could and could not do. For his part, the liquidator explained, in the best legal tones, that as an officer of the court he could only do what was in the best commercial interests of the creditors and could not become involved in a battle between the men and the Government.

As they left the accountant's office they told the reporters: 'We have told him we will try to keep him out. He can do his business from his own office.' After tempers cooled it was decided however that he would be allowed to work from the Linthouse administrative H.Q. of the company. It was felt that at this stage of the conflict it was wiser policy to ignore rather than obstruct his work.

Over the next few days there was a euphoric uncertainty about the situation. Although the takeover had openly been discussed since the crisis broke on 11 June there were very few hard plans in existence.

The idea of taking over the yards and keeping the men at work after they had been paid off by the liquidator had first been proposed at a meeting of the full complement of stewards in the Glasgow Trades Council Club on 13 June by Scotstoun convener Sam Barr. He had arrived at this concept after talks with union colleagues. His union was the Amalgamated Society of Boilermakers, Shipwrights, Blacksmiths and Structural Workers and they stood to lose many of the 5,000 members who worked in U.C.S.

At first the idea was not too well received. Some classed it among the dreams, and not the possibilities, of protest. But after discussion it was accepted as the general policy of the shop stewards.

So when the takeover took place there were still some who doubted if a 'work-in' could be practical. It took long discussions to evolve the practice of running a 'work-in'. Problems were raised almost at once at departmental meetings throughout the yards and brought back to the co-ordinating committee.

The problems were mainly mundane, the political theory being universally accepted. The men wanted to know about insurance cards, redundancy money and accident insurance. At first questions on this were answered by James Airlie, the chairman of the co-ordinating committee with, 'Don't worry, we'll deal with that when the time comes.'

As, in the following weeks, each of the problems became pressing, the committee dealt with them with almost casual coolness.

Should the men keep their redundancy money, often amounting to several hundred pounds? It was decided that any man laid off by the liquidator should take his redundancy money. There was a danger that when the liquidator asked for men to volunteer for redundancy that the financial attraction might break the solidarity. In the final analysis few chose to give up work for the redundancy money. In the depression of Clydeside 1971, jobs were very valuable.

Another problem was whether the men should sign on at the Labour Exchange and take their unemployment benefit. This would have placed less of a burden on the stewards' Fighting Fund. On that problem, it was decided that if the men signed on at the Buroo (a Scots diminutive of the thirties title of the Bureau of Employment) they were accepting the redundancies. The committee's policy was to ignore redundancies and if a man received his cards then he should hand them over to the stewards.

The cards were stamped 'self-employed' after much debate with the local employment exchange on whether the committee could technically become the men's employers.

Insuring the men who 'worked-in' against accident was the thorniest problem. The insurance obtained by Mr. Smith did not cover people he did not employ, so the yard conveners tried as best as possible to direct their men to the less dangerous parts of the yard, though it was not always possible.

Whenever the problem was raised with Airlie he replied: 'Well, tell them not to have any accidents!'

It was decided that the men should have their average take-home pay, based on their previous six months earnings. This fact was kept secret by the stewards because it was feared that when people giving to the

Fighting Fund found the U.C.S men were getting higher wages than themselves it would cause dissension. On the other hand it was argued the men could hardly attack the Government's suggestion that the wages be lowered if the first to do just that were the men themselves.

If the redundancies were to be ignored, normal working had to be the policy and that meant normal wages.

In any case the Fighting Fund did not pay all of the men's wages. Most of the unions with members in the yards - fourteen in all - decided to pay their men dispute benefit. (At first unemployment benefit had been offered but was rejected as implying an acceptance that the men no longer worked for U.C.S.).

This meant that the Fighting Fund, which had already received large donations from these same unions, only had to make up part of the men's pay. On average £5 was paid in dispute benefit.

Each morning after the takeover the committee met in the classroom in Clydebank. The room was designed like crew quarters deep in the hold of a ship. It was painted in functional green and was lined on one side with a row of wash-hand basins and mirrors. Weird pipes from the stifling Heath Robinson ventilation system - probably rescued from a pre-war liner - twisted round the ceiling.

On the blackboard throughout the months of the campaign, alongside the Fund appeal posters, were two triangular diagrams. On each side of one were the words, 'heat, fuel, oxygen' and round the other 'cooling, smothering, starving'. It was not a political slogan.

Each morning the committee met there to consider action, hear reports of meetings held all over Britain, or to receive hundreds of visitors. Within a week of the takeover, they were visited by world journalists, film crews, political party leaders, trade unionists, even a sculptor.

Chairman each morning was James Airlie, who had served on the committee since the mid-sixties. He was a thirty-four-year-old engineering steward from

Govan. He was also an ex-military policeman and it showed when he chaired meetings. Decisions were taken quickly and deviations from the stewards' policy - or party line - were not easily tolerated.

Along with Jimmy Reid he was a member of the executive of the Scottish Communist Party and is very much in the hard mould of Clydeside Communists. Yet beneath the tough exterior he assumed, there were often touches of intelligent humour.

He was at his best when picking off witty points from the weaknesses, mainly political, of other workers. He used this technique especially when under pressure to win his audience over. For there was a political purpose to everything he did.

He and Reid are the kind of people who have politics in every vein, every muscle of their bodies. Reid, too, is of the same hard Clydeside mould, though he translates that hardness into better and more powerful language.

Unlike Airlie, the industrial strong man, Reid was the political force of the co-ordinating committee. His most active working years have been spent as a full-time political organiser with the Communist Party - including a spell as General Secretary of the Scottish Communist Party - and he only returned to the yards in 1969.

Now thirty-nine years old with a handsome, wild Scottish face there is still a lot in him of the young fifteen-year-old who threw in a job in the Scottish Stock Exchange for a more 'honest' job as an engineering apprentice.

He has an unceasing urge to be politically active and, both on leaving the army after his national service and on leaving full-time organising, he was elected shop steward within six weeks of starting work.

The U.C.S. campaign has elevated him to a position of national standing. He is well known for his brilliant oratory, which combines moral strictures with a tendency to prick pompous politicians and their pompous deeds with witty comparisons drawn from the telly world.

To the delight of headline writers he makes remarks

James Reid

John Davies and James Reid

about the Government such as the Al Capone/Boy Scout comparison. He also said, they 'believe in the economics of Alice in Wonderland' and are 'an 007 Government with a licence to kill industry'.

The men who drew up the report suggesting closing the yards had written a 'political obscenity. Compared to these men the editors of OZ look like re-incarnated Godfrey Winns'. The appointment of an insurance tycoon as head of the new company was, to Reid, 'more reminiscent of Monty Python's Flying Circus than a shipbuilding board'. All off the cuff.

A light comes into his eyes on a platform that is only half there off it. For he is also an ambitious man who has no doubts that he has the right to speak for his brothers. He has that arrogance of the Left that brooks no opposition, especially from the Left, and modesty would be a pretence on his part.

Much of the success of the U.C.S. publicity machine can be attributed to Reid alone and there is no doubt that he contributed much to the despair that covered John Davies' face whenever he came to Glasgow.

There was however more strength in the co-ordinating committee than just these two men who bore the brunt of the publicity glare that shone on U.C.S. continually. There were alongside them over twenty men who could address mass meetings and put across the arguments with equal feeling if not with quite as much skill.

The committee became, in effect, a body of full time revolutionaries, spending their time travelling throughout Britain speaking to hundreds of workers and creating the enormous support that the campaign received.

There were men like Sam Barr, the Communist convener at Scotstoun, like Willie McInnes and Bob Dickie, who were equally militant but felt uncomfortable in party confines. They were three totally genuine, passionate, if quiet, men.

There were also older stewards who had seen many crises, like the indestructible Gerry Ross, the Clydebank boilermakers convener, who never once smiled during the many months of private meetings I attended. You knew without asking that he felt this was not a time for laughing and that was that. In any case true revolutionaries don't smile.

There were others like Willy Holt and Sam Gilmore, whose trip to Wales to address three meetings turned into a marathon of over twenty meetings when word of their speaking ability got about. Like Roddy McKenzie who would be proud, I am sure, to be called the meanest, and friendliest, treasurer around.

Their common bonds were their class, their country, their comitment. But above all this was their knowledge, either personally or through their fathers, of what tough times meant in shipbuilding.

Willie McInnes speaks for many when he says: 'I was born in the Depression in 1930. My father came back from the First World War to look for a better life. But for eighteen years he never worked, and we had thirteen of a family.

'The day my father died in the bedroom, my sister was born in the kitchen and we had to get in what they called the Parish Doctor.

'There's a tradition when someone sees a kid for the first time of giving it a couple of bob. Well, my cousin came in and gave my mother half-a-crown for the kid. She went out and bought sausages for us. That was our meal.

'When my father died my mother had to go out and work morning and night to raise us, without any help from the state.

'She was deprived of parish clothes, everything, because my father hadn't worked.

'Maybe it's made me a wee bit bitter but I always say that my kid will never go through that.'

When Willie McInnes said that there were 135,000 people in Scotland without a job - 6.3 per cent of the population. There were areas, like Springburn in Glasgow, where the number of men without a job was one in five.

In September 1971 there were 133,600 people chasing the 8,154 jobs which were available.

Throwing another 6,000 men onto that list would

have been a disaster for Scotland. How had one of its proudest industries reached the edge of collapse. Why had these men taken up arms against the Government?

It's a long story.

II

A MAGNUM OR A MINIATURE?

Upper Clyde Shipbuilders Ltd. was formed as a result of Government policy. Its constituent parts were not, however, forced together; they were bribed into a merger.

The birth of the consortium was a last attempt to halt the decline of power in the shipbuilding industry, not only of Upper Clyde, but of Britain. After the war, Britain had a ship-building bonanza.

The Allies had bombed the prospect of post-war German and Japanese competition out of the market. We had a massive slice of the world market and ships slid down the slipways with profitable regularity.

But by the beginning of the sixties, the long term results of the 1939-45 war began to show. The bombs had been directed at foreign shipyards, but they might just as well have been dropped on many British yards. For the Germans and Japanese had started up their shipbuilding industries again and the yards which had been flattened were rebuilt and modernised to an extent never undertaken in Britain.

New machinery and methods, coupled with massive economies of scale, produced flow line production enabling these countries to consistently underprice British yards. In sharp contrast to this modernisation, the British industry struggled on with old capital equipment.

It has been estimated that the purchase of new equipment for the whole industry in the fifties was about £4 million to £5 million a year compared with the loss of £9 million annually through normal usage.

A report by the Department of Scientific and

Industrial Research in the late fifties, stated that money spent on research and development was just over the £250,000 mark per annum. When the experimental tank at Clydebank is closed, there will be one, Government-owned, tank for the whole British industry. The obstinate refusal to re-invest some of the large profits from the fat years led to some very hard times.

In 1950, 48 per cent of the ships launched in the world were built in Britain. By 1960, it was 16 per cent, by 1964, it was down to a sad 6 per cent. By then yards were going to the wall - on Upper Clyde, Denny's, Simons-Lobnitz, Harland and Wolff, Barclay Curle, all sank.

Between 1950 and the creation of the U.C.S., the number of yards on the river fell from twenty-eight to seven.

When the Lithgow family pulled out of a bankrupt Fairfields yard in Govan, Glasgow, to concentrate on their profitable yards on the Lower Clyde in 1965 the message finally got through.

The threat of 3,000 jobs being lost forced Government and private enterprise together. A new company was set up under Scots industrialist Sir Iain Stewart as chairman. The new company was a complete breakaway from anything known before in the industry. None of the traditional shipbuilding families were present. Instead there was an amalgam of capital and labour, the first represented by insurance millionaire Hugh Stenhouse and Stewart himself, the chairman of Hall-Thermotank and vice-chairman of Scottish Television; the other side were represented on the board by Lord Carron, president of the Amalgamated Engineering Union and Andrew Cunningham, a district secretary of the General and Municipal Workers Union.

In addition there were experts in every aspect of modern management and productivity techniques. These included Professor Ken Alexander, of the Department of Economics at Strathclyde University, Sir Jack Scamp, the motor industry's trouble shooter, and Jim Houston, an expert in productivity who came

25

over from Singer Sewing Machines.

The traditional families of the Clyde looked askance at this new arrival and none of the new attitudes or methods rubbed off. It is said that one elderly shipbuilder threw his hands up in horror at the news of the appointment of Sir Jack Scamp. He was under the impression that the Labour Government had appointed Communist dockers' leader Jack Dash to the board. But if the established builders were not happy, others were. The unions had long been impatient to get round the table with management and hammer out a future for the industry. The 'Fairfields Experiment' was the first to let them do it.

Joe Black, the chairman of the Clyde District Committee of the Confederation of Shipbuilding and Engineering Unions remembers bitterly the frustration he had felt before then, as yards were closing and his members were being thrown out of work. 'In 1965, we went to the Clyde Shipbuilders Association and said bluntly: "You have a productivity problem, we have a wages problem. Let's marry them. Let's introduce method study and work measurement to the shipyards." But the Clyde shipbuilders said this was impossible, that these techniques could not be applied to shipbuilding.

'What they meant was, of course, that they didn't understand these problems and consequently wouldn't apply the solutions. We were talking to the Clyde shipbuilders about critical path analysis and they thought we were talking about a Greek tanker owner.'

The Government held half the equity of the new company and the unions and private capital held the rest. Some unions had to change their constitutions to allow them to make such an investment. For the next two years the Govan Yard was a centre of attention for the industry. The whole organisation and structure of the yard was turned upside down as Houston and his assistants set about introducing those methods the Clyde shipbuilders had rejected. Outwardly the results were good. Strikes were reduced as a result of the greatly improved industrial relations system centred on the Central Joint Council where management

26

and unions sat down to discuss policy for the first time. The Fairfields Procedure Agreement stated: 'The Company undertakes to keep the men well informed about the Company, its prospects, trading conditions and policies.' Productivity shot up. The number of hours lost through strikes fell from 96,000 in 1965 to 24,000 in 1966.

The Company was thought to be making a profit by 1968. Unfortunately there has never been a definitive assessment of the success or otherwise of Fairfields. Despite the above successes, there is the certain fact that some of the losses inherited by U.C.S. came from the Govan concern. The Jervis Bay which was completed a year late, at a cost of over £1 million to U.C.S., was inherited from Fairfields. Ironically, the experiment came to an end as a result of an attempt by the Government to repeat the Fairfield's formula in the rest of British shipbuilding.

In February 1965, Douglas Jay, President of the Board of Trade, had appointed the Shipbuilding Inquiry Committee under R.M. Geddes to examine the industry. It reported fifty-three weeks later. The Geddes report stated: 'It is, in our view, no accident that the leading foreign firms are those who attack the growing world market and operate on a large scale. The starting point has to be the structure of the industry.

'Success in the world market requires the re-deployment and more intensive use of resources rather than a reduction of capacity. Firms should be big enough to enjoy the real benefits of scale.' A 'fresh start' was needed, said Geddes, and that would require 'a kind of organisation and a kind of management, both general and specialist, new to the industry or at any rate equal to the best already in it. A lot of give and take will be required from the present shareholders, directors and senior managers if the changes are to be made... They will need new money and some new men to get the benefits quickly and so to convince themselves and others that a fresh start has been made. '

For the Clyde, said Geddes, there was a case for two groups because of the physical distances between some of the yards on the Upper and Lower reaches. Of

Upper Clyde and Clydebank, he said: 'To attack the growing world market (they) would have to consider how much attention the sophisticated end of the market would justify.'

From Geddes stemmed a Shipbuilding Industry Bill which Anthony Wedgwood Benn, the new Minister of Technology, piloted through Parliament unopposed. The Act created the Shipbuilding Industry Board which had the power and funds to give credits to shipowners as well as aid to yards merging or modernising. The large sum of £200 million was made available for credits which were in effect a Government subsidy to shipowners placing orders with British yards. The buyer received credit at low rates of interest to enable him to place the order. Although it is in theory an arrangement between the shipowner and the Government, the yard is very much an interested party. For the Government can say to a shipowner: 'We will give you credit, but not for that shipyard' - a situation which happened in 1970 to U.C.S.

The rush to collect the re-organisation and expansion grants was tremendous. Yarrow's, Stephen's of Linthouse, and Connell's of Scotstoun, were the first to discuss the merger. Brown's and Fairfield's saw no alternative but to join in. The Shipbuilding Industry Board supervised the merger. The new three-man board was chaired by Sir William Swallow, a former head of Vauxhall Motors, and its members were Mr. Anthony Hepper, a former managing director of Thomas Tilling Ltd., the makers of Pretty Polly stockings and tights, and Joe Gormley, an executive member of the National Union of Mineworkers. Hepper headed a three-man committee set up by the S.I.B. to supervise the formation of U.C.S. He was helped by banker A.W. Giles and management consultant J.H.F. Macmichael.

Everybody won a prize. Hepper became the chairman and managing director of the new company. John Brown's received 30 per cent of the shareholding. The loss-making yard was at long last unburdened by the otherwise successful John Brown parent company

28

and taken under the wing of the new subsidised company. During the next year the profits for the John Brown Group without Clydebank went up from £2,362,121 to £4,544,877. Stephen's received a 10 per cent shareholding for their failing yard. Sir Eric Yarrow managed to swing a very beneficial deal whereby he came into the new company but remained largely independent. His yard, which specialised in naval contracts, was still owned by a separate company known as Yarrow (Shipbuilders) Ltd., but 51 per cent of the shares were owned by U.C.S. For these shares he received £1 million and 20 per cent of the shares of U.C.S.

Connell's, the smallest yard, did exceptionally well. They had a 5 per cent holding worth £200,000 but in addition they were paid £4000,000 for profits they predicted would come from £14 million worth of orders they had already taken and which would now be built by U.C.S. They were also guaranteed a commission on any new orders which Sir Charles might bring to the new company. He claimed that since he was a shipowner as well as builder, he was entitled to a payment from any orders his companies placed with U.C.S. There were other companies named by Connell's as being ones over which they had influence and from whose orders they would also expect commission.

Fairfields, as well as being the largest shareholder at 35 per cent of the £4 million issues share capital, received a cash payment to their own shareholders. Stewart however only stayed with the new company for a matter of weeks before resigning over the non-appointment of Jim Houston to the position of Management Services Director. He felt that this was an indication of how the new board viewed his individual management philosophy and he has since been scathing of the U.C.S. approach to industrial relations and productivity.

The new board was large and composed almost entirely of former directors of the five yards. Hepper was Chairman. There were two deputy chairmen, Connell and Yarrow. The S.I.B. appointed a canny

Scots accountant Alexander Mackenzie as their director. Fairfields nominated Professor Alexander in place of Stewart. Other directors were: T.H. Burleigh, John Rannie, John Starks, and R.A. Williamson, all of John Brown's; management consultant M.O. Hughes; James F. Stephen, chairman of Alexander Stephen and Sons; James Corfe, marketing expert from Shell; James Duff, production director, who came from English Electric; and H.L. Farrimond, a former I.C.I. man. Andrew Hargrave of the Financial Times a few months later commented on 'dynastic rivalries which were bound to make co-operation in a single merged unit extremely difficult.'

The unions, too, were happy. Within a month of starting up the new company granted them a concession never before given on the Clyde. There was to be a three-year guarantee of work for the labour force. Dan McGarvey, the tough, blunt president of the Amalgamated Society of Boilermakers, the largest U.C.S. union, sat down at the negotiating table with the elegant Mr. Hepper. When they stood up, the stocking manufacturer had been baptised into the world of ship-building by a spray of rhetoric from McGarvey and the unions had won an outright victory. There was to be no laying off between ships, the root cause of unrest and insecurity in past decades.

It meant though that the order book now had always to be full to keep the large labour force occupied. So Hepper set off round the world taking each and every order he could get, often on the tightest profit margins. It was a policy which contributed to many of the subsequent financial problems. At the time it seemed there was nothing else that could be done but the sudden steep inflation of the next few years caught U.C.S. in a tight grip and meant that ships were being built for prices below the cost of production. It meant too that Hepper had to take each and every order he could get and the order book had a jumbled appearance with ferries, tankers, dredgers and other specialised ships all mixed together. There was no freedom to introduce standardisation. Geddes' warning that the company would have to rethink the advisability of remaining at the sophisticated end of the market had to be put to one side.

There wasn't much cheering at the launch in February 1968 but there was a quiet optimism, especially among the supporters of Geddes. A £3½ million champagne bottle had been smashed across its bow by the S.I.B. Another £2 million was promised for any large capital expenditure on modernisation. Everyone hoped it had been baptised with a magnum. In the subsequent years of inflation it proved to be a miniature.

By March 1969, the company was short of working capital and the S.I.B. gave another £3 million grant to cover the shortage. To the nervous suppliers of Clydeside it was a danger sign. They had already had their fingers burned in several bankruptcies on Clydeside in the past few years. Within weeks the company was under heavy pressure from creditors.

In April, the company again turned to the S.I.B. for help and were told that any further money would have to be offset by higher productivity, more effective management, a trimming of the workforce and a blitz on absenteeism, which was then running at about 9 per cent. To meet this, a corporate plan by which U.C.S. would reach profitability by 1972-73 was produced for the company by the P-E Consulting Group. It detailed proposals to increase steel production at Clydebank, Govan and Scotstoun divisions in conjunction with the closure of Linthouse as a shipbuilding yard. No plans for a rundown of the labour force were mentioned, the Linthouse staff being absorbed elsewhere.

The unions and management met with Benn in the Central Hotel on 7 May 1969. Benn was in an uncompromising mood, and displayed none of the sweet reason of the press conferences. He told both sides that the Corporate Plan was unacceptable. The main stumbling block was the proposal that the Government should attack the creditor pressure by guaranteeing the company for a five-year period. Benn listed the help the Government had given Upper Clyde in the past few years. This was: - £24 million for **QE 2**; over £1 million for Fairfields; £1.7 million as part of the development area policy; payment of 40 per cent of all capital investment; the £5 million inaugural loan from the S.I.B.; and the £3 million in March.

There were two reasons, said the Minister, for refusing such a guarantee. First, other shipbuilders would demand similar aid if they saw Upper Clyde in a trading position where it could afford to take loss-making orders knowing that the Government would make up the difference. Second, such a guarantee would result in wage negotiations being carried out by both sides in a 'climate of knowledge' that the company could afford to go into a loss to meet a heavy claim.

And he ended bluntly: 'The Corporate Plan is not on. The responsibility for the future lies with the U.C.S. management and the workforce. There won't be a long term if the short term remains so bad.'

That week, Alistair Warren, editor of the Glasgow Herald wrote a scathing editorial on the failure, as he saw it, of the S.I.B. to provide adequate working capital. He wrote:

Because of a lack of working capital which was not and could not have been foreseen when the group was formed early last year, U.C.S. has been brought to the brink of liquidation; indeed on at least one occasion in recent weeks the threatened postponement of a launch because of wind conditions would have meant, it if had materialised, that a payment to U.C.S. would have been withheld and there would not have been enough money in the kitty to pay the week's wages.

A fine way this to have to run a major unit in what is still one of Britain's most important exporting industries.

On 30 May, Hepper told the unions: 'The financial situation is deteriorating rapidly. The company is on a knife edge with creditors making constant and daily demands. A writ by a creditor now would create

32

the final crisis.' What the company wanted, said
Hepper, was £5 million for capital investment and
£7 million to £8 million for working capital. The
Government offer of £9 million left a £3 million gap
which had to be bridged.

Benn came back to Glasgow again on 6 June at the
height of the crisis. Now it was not only money
problems which faced U.C.S. Sir Andrew Crichton,
the buyer of the Jervis Bay, was understandably
worried about the ship's delay and was threatening
to tow it to Germany for completion. The morale and
reputation of the company would never have recovered
from such an event. The order book, too, was shaky
with only one new order so far that year. Again Benn
stuck to his offer, £5 million for capital expenditure,
but only £4.3 million for working capital. For this
further money, said Benn, the S.I.B. wanted 'real
shipyard experience' on the Board. Manpower would
have to be reduced as well.

All day long the directors, the unions, and a large
press corps sat about the St. Enoch Hotel, in Glasgow,
in different rooms, as Benn flitted between them. By
6 p.m. the position had not advanced. The possibility
of a 10 per cent or $7\frac{1}{2}$ per cent wage cut across the
board had been put to the union side of the Joint Council
who had refused to discuss it. By 8 p.m., the
directors gave in. They told Benn they would try to
find the other £3 million elsewhere, knowing within
themselves it would be almost impossible. The unions
agreed to talk about manpower reductions. In the next
twelve days Hepper approached over forty sources in
Britain and on the continent for money without
success and on 17 June admitted that the money was
not going to be found. The board told Benn that in the
light of both the S.I.B. statement that it would be
prepared to discuss 'the developing financial situation'
early in 1970, and the union willingness to discuss
manpower, they felt they could survive, in the short
term, on the £9.3 million. As a concession the
S.I.B. agreed to divide the same total differently,
making £5 million the sum for working capital. In
giving the money the S.I.B. required a capital

reconstruction which gave it a 48 per cent holding in the company. With the 1½ per cent union shareholding it meant that indirect control had now become more or less direct.

Many of the directors resigned as part of the company's plan to streamline its organisation. Mr. Hubert Farrimond, the highly respected personnel director said on resigning: 'It seems to me that the U.C.S. board are no longer in effective control because of the financial situation.' He obviously felt that the S.I.B. were being too optimistic in their assessment of when the company would reach profitability for he added: 'There are known differences between the S.I.B. and the U.C.S. board on such things as the objectives, the time scale, and the methods of achieving objectives.' Other directors made similar statements.

The biggest change to come out of the re-organisation was the replacement of Hepper as Managing Director by Kenneth Douglas, the managing director of Austin and Pickersgill, the successful Wearside shipbuilders. The new board was Hepper, chairman; Douglas, Starks, Yarrow, Connell, Alexander, Hughes and Mackenzie.

Douglas breezed into U.C.S. like a gust of fresh air. He brought with him a strong reputation based on his successful introduction of both effective cost accounting and standardisation to Austin and Pickersgill. Like Yarrow, Connell and Stephen, his father and grandfather had been in shipbuilding. Unlike their ancestors his had been platers on Tyneside and had known years of unemployment in the thirties. Douglas himself started as an apprentice draughtsman at the age of sixteen. He had a tough approach across the bargaining table which earned the respect of the unions. McGarvey said when told of the appointment: 'They've made a good choice.'

On 14 July, Douglas came up to Glasgow to meet both the Board and the unions. He affirmed his faith in the industry and its long term future and assured them: 'I am certain the will to survive exists in U.C.S.' He went to some pains in his remarks to

stress that his was not a Government or S.I.B.
appointment but that he had come to the company at
the request of the Board of Directors. As he left a
reporter asked him if he was hopeful for the future
of the Clyde. He replied bluntly: 'I'm forty-eight. I
wouldn't have taken on a dead duck.'

Nor, presumably, a lame one.

III

PRAIRIE DOGS AND BEGGING BOWLS

There was a new captain on the bridge, but all was not plain sailing. Within a few months of receiving the £9.3 million the company again faced a working capital shortage. In December 1969 the Government kept their word of June with a further working capital injection of £7 million. It was more willing to hand out this sum than it had been to give the June loan because at last things seemed to be moving at U.C.S.

Management and unions had come closer together than they had been during the first eighteen months. At the start there had been a lot of unrest. Geddes himself had foreseen this when he provided grants for transition and merger. The lower-paid yards put pressure on to get parity with the better paid. But now the two sides set about creating a harmony. The Joint Monitoring Committee, which had been formed on the streamlining of the board, was a success.

Standardisation was brought in with a design for an 18,000 ton bulk carrier called the Clyde, and a Super Clyde at 26,000 tons. The loss-making ships taken on under Hepper began to work their way slowly out of the system.

But most of all, production was steadily going up. In 1968, three ships were delivered; in 1969, seven; and in 1970, twelve ships. The programme for 1971 was eighteen ships.

Under Douglas steel production rose from eleven tons per man per year to 23.6 tons. In the yards of Upper Clyde, in the fifteen years before its creation, the steel production figures had never risen above ten tons per man each year.

The steel production was helped by the change of the Linthouse division from a ship building yard to a production shop for making pre-assembly steel units.

The change was carried out at the same time as Douglas arrived. The administration, including a sophisticated computer system, was based at a new office complex in Linthouse and much of the administrative duplication between the four divisions was being cut away at long last.

The increase was not only a result of the drop in manpower among steel workers of 16 per cent and a among all U.C.S. employees of 25 per cent (about 4,500 workers), it also resulted from a gross increase in steel production. In 1970 the company produced 867 tons each week, by mid-1971 the figure was 1,300 tons. Douglas stated that the company's productivity evaluation set steel workers at 85 per cent and the outfitting trades not far behind that.

Union negotiations were greatly rationalised too. In the beginning, U.C.S. inherited 700 wage rates, three years later there were four. National amalgamations meant that the company had to negotiate with less unions representing more employees.

Strikes, which had mushroomed at the beginning of the company began to die away as, by spring 1971, the disparity of wages between the four divisions was being abolished.

The shop stewards, the men who usually took the blame for being obdurate in the face of advance and productivity, began to feel optimistic for the first time in a decade.

Clydebank steward James Reid was one. 'In the last year U.C.S. was recording progress in productivity that was unequalled in British shipbuilding. For the first time we had meaningful negotiations on production.

'Before that period they would just come to you and say "Come on lads, co-operate to complete this order and meet a delivery date", and then when the boat was delivered you were sacked. Now that's what I call a positive disincentive production. How could you talk about productivity in an industry like that?

'In the last year, we had established with the

management a phased programme of production which moved from one vessel to the next. In such circumstances you can start talking about productivity and we served on the committees and responded. The productivity records at the end were second to none in Britain. '

Douglas himself stated in a letter to The Times on 2 July: 'Labour relations have, according to the unions and their representatives, never been of a higher order and production is running at levels comparable with any British shipyard at this time, and this in spite of delays in materials and equipment due to the financial situation. '

Of his term in office from August 1969 to mid-July 1971, he added:

> During this period we, as a group of three ship-yards, will have launched twenty vessels and delivered nineteen, this coupled with a drastic reduction in the labour force of 25 per cent. This output is not based on producing standard ships, but includes naval vessels, a large passenger ship, container ships, dredgers, and oil drilling rigs (the first in the world), cargo liners and bulk carriers.
>
> In October 1970 we set our programme of launchings for 1971 at sixteen ships. To date we have launched six and with the two vessels to be launched on 14 July, we will have achieved eight launches virtually in half a year - an average of one ship every three and a half weeks. This has been achieved with complete co-operation between management and labour.

As well as the improved relations and productivity a basic cause of this change was the new company policy of operating the order book only two years in advance.

Professor Ken Alexander was one who advocated this policy on the Board. 'There was a general feeling that in a very rapid inflationary situation, it was wise if you could replenish your order book every two years, rather than for a four year period ahead because you would obviously get the prices wrong on that basis. Given the pace of inflation it was quite sensible. That is always assuming you are going to be continuously in business over the period.'

The basic problem throughout for U.C.S. still remained. Suppliers were still cautious and demanded speedy payment. There was still a shortage of working capital and the company continued to live a hand-to-mouth existence.

There was no illusion that the Government would not have to be approached for further help towards the 1972 goal of profitability. Indeed Treasury Minister Harold Lever had told Douglas in December 1969 when he gave the company £7 million directly from Government funds that the company would probably need a further £3 million within the next two years. They had hopes though that they might need no more than that.

But in June 1971, they went to the Government for £7 million. What followed is dealt with later in this book. Why, when everything was going so well, had the company reached this situation?

The beginning of the end dates back to October 1970 when, not the shortage of working capital, but another problem, beset U.C.S.

The prop of Government support in the form of credits to shipowners placing orders with the company was taken away. The Government had changed.

Conservative politicians did not like Upper Clyde Shipbuilders. There is no shortage of statements by front or back benchers to support this opinion. Mr. Heath himself, when Leader of the Opposition, had told millions of S.T.V. viewers in November 1969 that industry in Scotland didn't like the Labour Government's policy of subsidies through Investment Grants and the Regional Employment Premium. They did not, said Mr. Heath, want 'a soup kitchen economy in a soup kitchen country.' Older shipyard workers on Clydeside were in no doubt what he was getting at. They could remember soup kitchens.

Enoch Powell put it in more graphic terms than the

others, but he was only expressing the belief of most members of his party. In a speech in Glasgow at the height of the June 1969 crisis, he warned that 'no industry, no population can survive as pensioners of the rest of the country.' With Teddy Taylor sitting next to him, he painted a picture of the American desert where the tourists were banned from feeding the prairie dogs because if the dogs were to get accustomed to relying on the tourists, they would die when the winter came.

He went on: 'I mean no disrespect to the Clyde-siders when I say that the tale of the prairie dogs is very relevant to their predicament.'

He returned to the subject seventeen months later, again in Glasgow, when in an interview with Scottish political writer Stewart MacLachlan, he told the Scots to 'stop rattling your begging bowls' and advised the country's 99,000 strong army of unemployed 'don't look for Government hand-outs. Go somewhere else.

'If the people in Scotland depend on Government expenditure I am sorry for them. I am sure they would be more prosperous and happier if over the past twenty-five years the Government had not poured money into Scotland.'

There was another answer. 'I don't think that because Scotland has five million people it has a right to that size of population.' Asked if that meant Scotland could be faced with mass emigration he replied: 'If you don't like your geographical position - being away from the dense population markets - get out of it.

'But don't ask people to give you hand-outs. That's the begging bowl mentality.'

Despite the antipathy of the Conservative Party to supporting industry in general and U.C.S. in particular, not one M.P. voted against the Shipbuilding Industry Bill when it went through Parliament. That is not to say that support for it was unanimous. On the second reading of the Bill on 9 March 1967, two speeches of reservation were made.

The first was by another Conservative M.P. in Glasgow, the Hon. Tam Galbraith. Galbraith has represented Hillhead, a Tory stronghold for many years and in Macmillan's Government he was a junior minister at the Admiralty at the time of the Vassall case. He is the son of Lord Strathclyde who, at the age of eighty, still overshadows his son in the Scottish Conservative Party. His career in Parliament has been undistinguished. (Tam's unfortunate stiff-upper-lip style of speech once led a colleague of his to describe him to me as a 'ventriloquist's duck').

Galbraith attacked any question of subsidies for our shipbuilding industry - the only one left in the world unsupported by its Government. He said: 'if foreign countries are so stupid or generous as to offer ships at less than their true cost why do we not accept their bounty gratefully and encourage our shipping firms to buy in the cheapest market thus provided? This would obviously be good for the British shipping industry and the British taxpayer. Of course, if that happened, on any scale, it would probably sound the death knell of the British ship-building industry, at least on its present scale.

'Nevertheless,' said the ever-patriotic Tam, 'if it were the right thing for the nation, it might have to be faced.'

Similar to Galbraith in many respects, both in background and ideology is Old Etonian Nicholas Ridley, M.P. for Cirencester and Tewkesbury, younger son of Viscount Ridley, a director of a civil engineering contractors in north east England who said he would prefer, 'to achieve viable yards by means of letting inefficient and out-of-date units wither away... In my view, the best thing the Government could do would be to encourage the closure of the yards which are clearly getting into difficulty, thereby producing the men and the opportunity for other yards to expand and to make themselves viable.'

Ridley was not the front bench spokesman on ship-building at that debate but two years later he was the choice of Mr. Heath to make inquiries prior to formulating shipbuilding policy for the party before the 1970 election. Ridley therefore came to the Clyde to meet Sir Eric Yarrow in private on 3 December 1969. He met Hepper and Douglas and Scott-Lithgow, directors from the Lower Clyde, a month later. The notes which he prepared from these meetings and his suggestions as to policy have subsequently come to light and provide a frightening insight into Conservative thinking about a basic British industry.

The so-called 'Ridley Report' is in two sections. The first two pages concern the meeting with Yarrow. Ridley sent these notes in the form of a memorandum to Sir Keith Joseph, M.P., Miss Betty Harvie Anderson, M.P., Mr. Gordon Campbell, M.P. He told them that Yarrow's 'had suffered grievously through the merger, both in profits and in labour relations. They are being dragged down by this vast, loss-making and badly-run concern.' In fact it is now thought that Yarrow's had really been making losses all the years that civil service circles and west of Scotland industrial reporters had thought the firm to be profit making.

Ridley, as a result of this one-hour meeting, quickly arrived at 'The best long term solution', which was

Having regard to the politics of the situation as well as the economies:

a. Detach Yarrow's from U.C.S. and allow it to be independent prior to merging on agreed terms with Lower Clyde, or Thorneycroft.

b. For the Government (Labour or Tory) to bail out the rest of U.C.S. - to write off its debts, sell off Government shareholdings, close one or even two of its three yards, appoint a new chairman, and let it stand or fall on its own. This might cost £10 million but it would be the end of the nightmare.

c. To work towards an eventual merger of Lower Clyde, Yarrows, U.C.S.

According to Ridley the employment effects of this would be small with a workforce of only 5,000 remaining at U.C.S., a much expanded workforce of 6,000 at Yarrow's and another 1,000 being absorbed by Lower Clyde. This would only mean 1,000 on the dole!

He ended: 'The alternative is the continuance of huge losses, or the collapse of U.C.S. and 13,000 unemployed. I believe we should work out the scheme above in more detail. Get it agreed with all concerned, and then make it our policy.'

A month later Ridley again set out in a confidential document his impressions from a meeting with Douglas, Hepper, and, separately, some Lower Clyde directors.

This report noted: 'There has been little centralisation of facilities - only joinery shops and computers so far; and only little more planned. Other advantages claimed for the grouping of the five yards are a common labour policy, and the ability to take large orders. The advantages appear to be surprisingly small.' He also doubted whether the order book was large enough or would be profitable enough. He found that morale was bad and there was little managerial devolution.

Of Douglas he noted that he was not 'impressed'. Douglas when he saw the report said: 'The feeling is mutual'.

He reported that relations with Yarrow's were extremely strained. 'Eric Yarrow is publicly attacking U.C.S. and doing everything he can to extract Yarrow's from U.C.S.' In the conclusion he stated:

I believe that we should do the following on assuming office:

(i)   Give no more money to U.C.S.

(ii)   Let Yarrow leave U.C.S. if they still want to, and facilitate their joining Lower Clyde if they still wish to do so.

(iii)   This would lead to the bankruptcy of U.C.S.
We could accept this, in which case Lower
Clyde would take over one or two of the
yards.

Once again he claimed the employment effects would
be only 1,500 men looking for work. (The tables
with which he justified this claim defy explanation.
See Appendix).
   The sting was in the tail.

We could put a Government 'Butcher' to cut up
U.C.S. and to sell (cheaply) to Lower Clyde and
others, the assets of U.C.S. to minimise upheaval
and dislocation. I am having further views on the
practicality of such an operation which I will
report.

(iv)   After liquidation or reconstruction as
above, we should sell the Government
holding in U.C.S. even for a pittance.

Ridley suggested that this policy should not be made
public but that the Tories should confine themselves
to saying no money would be given by a Conservative
Government.
   He concluded: 'When we get in, we are clear to take
either of the courses set out in (iii) above. If U.C.S.
becomes viable, we merely adopt (iv). '
   So there it is. A plan for dismemberment of a
company employing people upon whom thousands more
depended.
   It would appear that Ridley's views hardened
further between the two meetings for, after the Yarrow
talk, he was all set for letting one or two yards
remain; its debts being paid by the Government; and
left to float with a labour force of 5,000 men. (Apart
from the size of the workforce, the proposal of the
'Four Wise Men'.)
   A month after stating this 'best solution' Ridley
advocated a complete closure. If Scott-Lithgow were
willing to take one or two of the yards, all would be

44

well. If not there would be closure and the selling off of the assets for a 'pittance' after his 'Butcher' had cut it up. No labour force was to be retained.

It seems strange too that Ridley should report both Hepper and Douglas as saying that the December 1969 loan of £7 million should be the last public money they would need. Both gentlemen had stressed to Lever and more or less got the promise that should it be needed, further money was likely to be forthcoming.

The really dramatic aspect of the document is the proximity it has in its advocacy to the events of 1971. It is of course only a small chink in the curtain. Ridley doubtless met many other persons in the shipbuilding industry on his policy-making inquiry. To assume that these documents are a true reflection of his thinking in 1971 would be unfair - as it changed from one month to the next, it could just as well have changed again.

However, it would appear that even if Ridley did modify his views, someone in Government stuck to them.

Was this report a blueprint for the Conservative Government? It is unlikely that it was. It is obviously an interim document and any final policy statement would be more polished and detailed. Also John Davies, the Secretary of State for Trade and Industry has denied seeing the document. Since he did not come into the inner decision making echelons of the Conservative Party till after the election, when Heath appointed him to the Cabinet, this is probably true.

I think the reason that the events have so neatly duplicated the suggestion lies in the character and, more important, the philosophy of both Davies and Ridley. Both are strict adherents to the non-intervention philosophy for industry. As Director General of the Confederation of British Industries Davies had for five years been a leading exponent of this philosophy. Ridley too is a fervent laisser-faire Conservative. So it makes no difference which of them saw the Upper and Lower Clyde shipbuilders, their ideology would have led them to these conclusions.

Or to put it another way. Either of them could have met nobody on Clydeside...and still have come to these conclusions.

IV

THE DECLINE INTO LIQUIDATION

When the Conservatives, after five summer months
of Government, finally found themselves faced with a
U.C.S. situation, it was, surprisingly, neither a
problem of shortage of working capital nor a request
for more funds from the company.

For the three years of its stormy life, the S.I.B.-
nominated director Alexander Mackenzie had sat
quietly on the U.C.S. board. As a chartered accountant
he saw his function in purely commercial terms. It
was his duty to protect the interests of the largest
shareholders, the S.I.B. and the Government, and
social or political considerations did not greatly
disturb him. That workers should cause industrial
unrest always eluded him.

The problems of a large workforce did not, as a
whole, intrude into the boardrooms of his other
companies. These were: Scottish Western Investment
Co. Ltd.; Second Great Northern Investment Trust
Ltd.; Glendevon Investment Trust Ltd.; London and
Montrose Investment Trust Ltd; London and Merchant
Securities Ltd.; Sceptre Investment Trust Ltd.;
Scottish Widows Fund and Life Assurance Society;
Sterling Trust Ltd.; Yarrow and Co. Ltd.

In October 1970, Mackenzie thought he saw a threat
to his shareholders' interests. The company was, he
considered, in danger of entering an illegal position,
that of trading in a situation where the company's
assets were worth less than the company's liabilities.
It was not a new fear - the company had on other
occasions felt itself skating perilously near liquidation.
Optimism plus nerve had at these times decided the

directors in favour of carrying on a few weeks more
in hopes of righting the situation, either through
Government or private aid.

Each time the gamble had paid off. This time too,
there were directors who would have counselled
another gamble. They never got a chance to, for
Mackenzie informed the S.I.B. of his fears without
telling the U.C.S. board what he was doing.

The Department of Trade and Industry instructed
the S.I.B. in October that credits for any shipowner
wanting to have a vessel built at U.C.S. should not
be given. No action was taken to change the situation
which Mackenzie said was threatening. Liquidation
could not of course be ordered until an examination
of the books showed an asset deficiency. Although the
Government or the S.I.B. could have ordered such
an examination none was ordered. If there was to be
a liquidation, the Government was not going to force
it. It would have to occur through the normal
processes of the market - that, after all, was the
philosophy.

The Minister responsible under Heath for U.C.S.
was John Davies. He had come into active politics
as M.P. for the county seat of Knutsford in Cheshire,
after a lifetime in the board rooms of Britain.
For five years in the early sixties he had been vice-
chairman and managing director of Shell-Mex and
B.P. Despite the fact that the company had a
substantial Government shareholding, Davies was
always a strong opponent of any Government
intervention. From 1965-69 he got his chance to put
his point across to the leaders of industry as the
Director General of the C.B.I. As a director of Hill
Samuel, and Black and Decker, he did not, naturally,
meet many Clydeside shipyard workers.

Parliamentarians as disparate as Enoch Powell
and Michael Foot have warned against the dangers of
appointing to Cabinet positions persons who have
reached their position in life by representing sectional
interests. Frank Cousins, the powerful leader of the
Transport and General Workers Union was a
parliamentary failure as Minister of Technology in the

Labour Government. Davies was taken from the opposite side of the fence to fill a similar position. Davies had been used to sitting down at a table with unions and hammering out agreements in the knowledge that eventually, no matter how tough the struggle, he would have to give a concession to make a gain. Now he was again sitting at that table but all the power was on his side. If he felt like it he could demand all the concessions he wanted.

To aid him, he had in his department Mr. Michael Noble as Minister for Trade and Sir John Eden, nephew of Sir Anthony Eden, as Minister of Industry. The Under-Secretary with responsibility for ship-building was none other than Nicholas Ridley!

On 14 October, Mackenzie had informed the S.I.B. of his fears. He was told then that the Department would have to consider the position on further credit guarantees. There were several applications in for orders worth £53 million and at least five owners were reaching completion of negotiations for these credits. Yet it was not till a fortnight later when Hepper was on the phone to the D.O.T.I. on 27 October about a different matter that he was told the credits had been stopped. He contacted Ridley, who told him officially that the Government was not satisfied the company could complete any order it might take.

This new affair obviously confirmed Mr. Davies in his industrial philosophy for a week later, on 4 November 1970, he produced the phrase which threatens to hang round the Government's neck like an albatross for the rest of its term of office. Winding up for the Government in the debate on Barber's 'mini budget' he proclaimed that the Government was gearing its policies to the 'great majority' who were not 'lame ducks, who do not need a hand, who are quite capable of looking after their own interests and only demand to be allowed to do so.' Was he thinking of U.C.S. when he said that 'national decadence' was to blame and that the vast majority did not live in a 'soft sodden morass of subsidised incompetence'. To emphasise he added: 'What is true of people is true no less of businesses. '

After that Hepper must have had little optimism when, on 19 November, the U.C.S. board submitted a plan to Ridley whereby the Government would agree to write down loans already given to the company in yet another capital reconstruction. The Under-Secretary said he would consider the idea. To sweeten the pill Hepper began approaching shipowners with ships being built at U.C.S. to ask them to agree to pay more than the agreed price for their ships. On 5 January 1971, the worried shipowners went to Davies to tell him they would pay 5 per cent more for their ships - a sum of £2.75 million - if he would agree to the capital reconstruction.

A week later the U.C.S. board finally agreed to the action which Hepper had hoped to avoid and Sir Eric Yarrow had worked for since mid-1969. They asked Davies to hive off Yarrow (Shipbuilders) Ltd. Although the company was a drain on U.C.S. funds it did afford protection to the company with its specialised market in naval contracts. The board had had no indication from Davies that he was going to accept the capital reconstruction suggestion. He had on 17 December rejected it and even after the promise of funds from the shipowners he would not commit himself.

The hiving off of Yarrow (Shipbuilders) was not a desire peculiar to the Conservatives. Harold Lever too had pressed on the company in December 1969 the idea of letting Yarrow's go. The separation was strongly advocated by the defence lobby in Whitehall, in both Governments. It was a complete negation of the Geddes idea for the Clyde since it created three Clyde groups.

On Tuesday, 2 February 1971 the Cabinet met. They decided that Yarrow (Shipbuilders) should be taken over by Yarrow and Company Ltd. The company were to be given a loan of £4½ million over three years. It was also agreed that credit guarantees for U.C.S. should be restarted.

Labour M.P.s approached Davies at midnight on the Tuesday after receiving a phone call from Glasgow to the effect that a large industrial concern on Clydeside was in difficulties and could be going into liquidation.

On the assumption it was U.C.S., Benn phoned Davies and Willie Ross saw Scots Secretary Gordon Campbell. They were assured that the second largest employer on Clydeside was not in danger.

What they did not know, but Davies knew well, was that the largest employer in the area - Rolls Royce - was in trouble. When the news of the R.R. crash came out later in the week the Labour M.P.s assumed the rumour they heard had concerned the aero engine firm. When U.C.S. went into liquidation itself in June, Scots Labour M.P.s, on discovering the long term effects of the October - February credits freeze, accused the Government of taking a political decision to continue the company for a few months because they could not afford the closure of two large Clydeside companies in one week. They also saw political motives in support for Yarrow's.

Sir Eric Yarrow has never been a darling of the Left. He is a well-known member of the Arms for South Africa lobby and his yard is now one of the few left in the world which is both technically able and politically free to build frigates for South Africa. Tribune M.P. Robert Hughes, North Aberdeen, attacked the Ministry of Defence loan to Yarrow (Shipbuilders). He said in the House of Commons: 'This was the great excuse we got from the Tories for not allowing Rolls Royce to go to the wall. It never ceases to astonish me that if the merchants of death want money there is no hesitation in finding it. If people are seeking money to provide weapons to kill people off in millions, there is a bottomless purse to provide that money.'

On 11 February, Davies announced to the House of Commons the hiving off and the £4$\frac{1}{2}$ million loan. He told them that Yarrow and Company Ltd. were 'acquiring' the 51 per cent shareholding of Yarrow (Shipbuilders) in U.C.S. He did not mention that the shares were bought from U.C.S. for £1. The transaction meant also that U.C.S. lost the only piece of major capital equipment created in its three year history - the £1.25 million covered berth at Yarrow's. Hugh MacPherson, political correspondent of the Spectator, voiced a suspicion in June that 'far from being hard-headed they (the Government) have feather-bedded certain private sectors' and described the new Yarrow group as 'the best stuffed lame duck in the land'.

In response to the minister's announcement of the hiving off as well as the capital reconstruction involving the writing down of much of the loans William Ross asked: 'Does the Government share the view of the U.C.S. directors who are confident that they will achieve viability?' Davies replied that the likelihood of viability was the view of the Board and added 'I have no view on the subject at all. If I were to have a view about the viability of every company in this country, I should indeed be perplexed.'

The House did not press the point that unlike most companies in the country, this one had as its major shareholder Mr. Davies himself and that many millions of public money was involved in it. The M.P.s were anxious to get on that day with the following debate on the Second Reading of the Rolls Royce (Purchase) Bill.

It seemed that U.C.S. was once again off a hook. Credits were being resumed, extra monies were due to come in from shipowners and the company was off again. But the five months without credits had left their toll. Worst, and first, hit was that old bugbear, working capital. Word had quickly gone round the shipping world that the credits had been stopped and the company found it difficult to get payments for instalments on ships. In October the cash flow deficit had been £165,000 in a company with a weekly turnover of over £1 million.

By February 1971 the company was running a deficit of over £6 million, as a result of the lack of payments through the winter and there was tremendous creditor pressure on them. They tried to struggle on but by June the crunch came and once again Hepper had to appeal for help from the Government.

On Wednesday 9 June the board met and considered their situation. They were in debt to the tune of over £4 million and were now being advised by their accountants that there was no guarantee that the wage bill of £250,000 a week could be met for very much longer. Hepper contacted Davies and appraised him of the extent of the debt - between £4 million and £5 million - which they estimated would be incurred by the end of August. The chairman told him that the company felt that the Government would have to inject £5 million to £6 million, mainly in the form of a grant, to keep the company going.

Davies discussed the situation with the Cabinet and told Hepper on the Thursday that to give the Government breathing space to consider action, he would guarantee the next week's wage bill and asked the board to 'hold their hand' for a few days. As the Cabinet met, the company was handing over the first of the 'Clyde' ships to be completed, the Sig Ragne, to Liverpool Liners Ltd. The Temple Hall was delivered on the same day.

On Friday 11 June, the workers in U.C.S. first became aware officially of the board's appeal to the Government for £5 million or £6 million in the form of an equity or grant. The officials had been uneasy all that week as various signs of crisis appeared. On the Thursday, staff in the Govan paint shop phoned round Glasgow trying to find a supplier who would send paint without demanding that cash be paid before handing it over. Hepper told the unions that he had asked for the money but that it looked as though the Government were going to prove very tough to convince. He phoned various Government and company officials well into Friday evening in an attempt to assess the situation.

The Glasgow Herald broke the story exclusively on the Saturday. Their industrial reporter Ian Imrie wrote of the tragedy of the situation at a time when U.C.S. was beginning to break through after a period of financial difficulty. He wrote: 'While U.C.S. were given assurances of about £20 million of Government aid the recurring difficulties appeared to arise from their receiving too little money, too late. '

It was a phrase which had been used by most Scots industrial reporters over the three years of U.C.S. An editorial on the front page argued for a reprieve for the company. It stated: 'The economic and social cost - never mind the political cost - of allowing U.C.S. to go to the wall would be vastly greater than £6 million. And to do so at a time when great strides are being made in the yards would be a cruel blow to the morale of management and workpeople throughout the region. '

By Saturday, Hepper had a detailed enough picture of the company's financial position to realise that the wage bill for even that next week could not be met. He flew down to England and met Davies on Sunday at the Minister's country home in Knutsford, Cheshire. He told Davies that unless the £6 million was forthcoming by Monday, the company would have no choice legally but to petition for a provisional liquidator. Davies went to Chequers to see Heath where they agreed that the company should be allowed to go into liquidation.

The next day Davies told the House of the events of the past few days. He said that the board had told him it still had hopes of attaining viability but was unable to forecast when the excess of liabilities might be reversed. True to his style, he added: 'The Government's judgment is that this company in its present grouping, saddled as it is with debt and dogged by deficit since its inception, having absorbed and lost some £20 million lent and guaranteed to it under arrangements made by the former Government, is unlikely to achieve a state of stability and prosperity without having repeated recourse to Government aid. '

The decision, said Davies, was 'that nobody's interest will be served by making the injection of funds into the company as it now stands. ' At this the Opposition benches erupted. Andrew Faulds, as usual, led the shouting. 'Disgraceful, bloody disgraceful. You're a disastrous Minister, ' he shouted. In face of the wall of noise from the Labour side of the House, Davies tried to struggle on with his prepared statement.

54

Eventually Govan M.P. John Rankin, on a point of order, asked that he repeat his last few sentences. A Labour back bencher cried out 'From disastrous'.

In the interests of ensuring the 'minimum dislocation'* of production and to preserve as much employment and assets as possible, the Government intended that a regrouping of the company should take place with the approval of the liquidator. To this end, said the Minister, he would appoint a group of experts to make proposals for action.

For twenty-five minutes the two sides of the House questioned the Minister, though most of the questions were less designed to elicit information than to score party points. Typical was the intervention of Tam Galbraith, many of whose constituents worked in the yards. He asked: 'Is my Right Hon. Friend aware that to all fair-minded people, his statement, which must have taken a great deal of courage to make, is a realistic way of dealing with the great industrial and human problem which has existed ever since this unnatural company was set up as a result of Socialist legislation?'

Harold Wilson ended question time by asking the Leader of the House and 'the part-time Prime Minister' to arrange an early debate. The M.P.s then went on to debate the Second Reading of the Education (Milk) Act which required the children of the unemployed to produce a medical certificate before receiving free school milk. The doctors of Clydebank were going to be busy.

By 4 p.m. on the Monday, everybody knew the worst. For the stewards, the politicians and the 8,500 workers of U.C.S., it was the signal for the start of a massive political campaign; for the owners and workers - possibly as many as 20,000 - in the ancillary trades along Clydeside, the news was a hard blow. Yet again there was a yard in bankruptcy

---

*The words are a chilling echo of Ridley's recommendation that a 'Butcher' be sent in to 'minimise upheaval and dislocation'.

at a cost to the various engineering shops, paint firms, haulage contractors and even caterers, who had geared their own output to that firm. One fishmonger in Govan Road, Glasgow, was left with a bill for £700 of fish which he had supplied to the company's canteen.

Over 80 per cent of the supplies bought by U.C.S. were purchased locally from firms in the west of Scotland. There were 2,466 ordinary creditors who were owed the enormous sum of £16,827,000. Largest and worst hit was the British Steel Corporation. Their bills, including one for £1,096,651 were completely written off. As another favourite target for the lame duck hunters of the Conservative Party, the Scottish board of the B.S.C. could not have been happy at getting a sum like that added to their liabilities at a time when they were negotiating with a hesitant Government to bring a £1,000 million steel plant to Hunterston in Ayrshire.

The B.S.C. works at Cambuslang, just outside Glasgow, went on to short-time working within twenty-four hours of the U.C.S. liquidation. The works supplied 30 per cent of their output to U.C.S., a total of 75,000 tons each year and the 1,500 work force were changed from a seventeen-shift rota to thirteen shifts a week.

The list of creditors to Upper Clyde Shipbuilders reads like a miniature Register of Companies. The variety of debt owed by a company like U.C.S. is phenomenal. From the vast sums owed to the B.S.C. to the £1 owed to English Electric, there are few major British firms who escaped. Every major shipyard in Britain and some abroad was owed money by Upper Clyde.

The Government also lost out indirectly as well as its direct share loss. There was B.S.C.; Thomas Cook and Sons; B.R.S.; B.E.A.; Customs and Excise; H.M.S.O.; Mintech; N.C.L.; and the Post Office were all owed money. Glasgow and Clydebank local authorities were creditors too.

There was no organisation or business basic to Scotland that was not owed money. Every newspaper,

U.C.S. launching at Govan yard

The liquidator, Robert Courtney Smith

every heavy engineering works, most technical instrument makers; local stationers, printers, dairies, butchers, sawmills, the list is endless. And all these names on the list represented employment.

Donald Maxwell, director of the British Marine Equipment Council, said in a letter to the Glasgow Herald on 18 July:

> The true cost of salving and dismantling the U.C.S. will never be known, because too many imponderables are involved. The loss of both work and profit from cancellation of firm forward ship contracts is bound to come... suppliers' losses are not bounded simply by unpaid bills. An equal amount is represented by equipment completed but not delivered by mid-June, some of which will be quite unsaleable elsewhere. While something like four times that figure is involved in orders in hand on which varying amounts of material has already been purchased.

With the appointment, after Davies' statement, of Robert Courtney Smith, the man who had organised the liquidation six years earlier of the Fairfield-Rowan engineering works, as the provisional liquidator for U.C.S. the history of Upper Clyde Shipbuilders Ltd. was officially finished.

The workers of U.C.S. had something else to say about it.

V

'WE DON'T ONLY BUILD BOATS...'

John Davies was not having the best of days. He had
made an unfortunate speech when opening the six and
a half hour Commons debate on U.C.S. In it he
touched briefly on the history of the company since
October when he had been forced to cut off the credits.
This he had done, he said, because he had
'responsibility for ensuring not only that the shipowners themselves are credit worthy in this respect
but that there is every reasonable prospect that the
ships in question will be delivered to them in due
time, and this prospect could not honestly be said to
be fulfilled at that time.'

He repeated that the company, to help resolve this
position, had suggested, the winter before the crisis,
that a capital reconstruction should be carried out.
In February 1971 he and his under-ministers had
been in no way critical of the re-construction. In
fact they had stated the proposal was the reason for
restoring the credits. He now had a different attitude
to the capital change.

He attributed the company's confidence then to both
the increased prices from the shipowners and the
Government's willingness to see 'substantially
written down' the £20 million or so which had, by
then, been lost. 'Its whole argument reposed on the
fact that we might as well accept the re-construction,
because the money had gone. We had no prospect of
anything other than that fact - that the money had gone -
so that we might as well accept the re-construction,
with a total write down.' The news the week before
had been a surprise to Mr. Davies apparently and he

59

had been unwilling, he said, to give money to a company whose short history had contained several similar instances.

It was neither a passionate nor compassionate speech. In a dry recitation of his facts there was little attempt to show at least a public sympathy for the people affected by liquidation. It dealt only with the hard facts of capital and none of the tragedy of labour. The words 'money', 'cash', 'sum', occur six times, 'financial' five times, 'profit' four times. But the words 'unions', 'redundancy', 'workers', 'men', 'unemployment', do not occur at all. The meaning of social consequences had still to be driven into Mr. Davies.

Wedgwood Benn, for the opposition, naturally blamed the Government for the situation. A lack of confidence, as a result of Conservative thinking, before and after the election had undermined the company. As examples he listed the Ridley 'Butcher' policy which had appeared in the Guardian first on 6 May 1970, the dismantling of the Industrial Re-organisation Corporation, the repeal of the Industrial Expansion Act which had financed the QE2, a speech by Davies to a Press Gallery lunch when the Minister had described the S.I.B. as a body 'designed to distort' the judgment of shipbuilders, and finally the credit freeze.

But Benn kept his revenge for the end of the speech. The day before, while under pressure, Davies had thrown a particularly damning quote at Benn. He had quoted the former Labour Minister as saying, 'After giving the most careful consideration to these proposals, the Government have regretfully concluded that, having regard to the need to contain Government expenditure, there is not sufficient priority to justify the investment of further public funds in this enterprise in the face of many competing demands on national resources' - (Official Report, 2 December 1969; Vol. 792, c.1305).

Benn now returned to this quote.

Mr. Benn: 'I take it that the argument is that having said that about U.C.S. it was hypocritical of me now to urge further support. I take it that was the point?'

Mr. Davies: indicated assent.

Mr. Benn: 'Did the Right Hon. Gentleman check the quotation personally?'

Hon. Members: 'Answer.'

Mr. Benn: 'I checked the quotation and the words were used on 2 December, not about Upper Clyde Shipbuilders but about the Beagle Aircraft Company.' (Hansard, Official Report, 15 June 1971; Vol. 819, c. 254-5).

Davies had been led gently into the Labour backbenchers' sights and they greatly enjoyed letting fly at their favourite target duck. It was not, perhaps, of great importance to the world at large but in Parliamentary terms it was a rough going over.

Scots M.P.s were naturally expected to fill the debate after the main speakers and, sure enough, first into the ring was Tam Galbraith, Tory M.P. for Glasgow, Hillhead. The son of Lord Strathclyde put on record the fact that 'as a Clydesider' it was with a heavy heart that he had to say that 'the day for reckoning had more than come'... 'This may mean a slimmer shipbuilding industry on the Clyde, and a tightening of our belts for a while.'

To his credit he was the only Scots Tory to speak in the debate from the backbenches.

After him came a long list of well known Clydesiders like Christopher Tugendhat (Cities of London and Westminster), Tom Boardman (Leicester South West), Stanley McMaster (Belfast East), T.H.H. Skeet (Bedford), John Biffen (Oswestry), Norman Tebbit (Epping), all speaking from the Government benches. Until Scottish Secretary Gordon Campbell closed the debate at 9.30 that evening not one other Scots Tory had shown an interest.

As the M.P.s were filing through the division lobbies a train carrying 400 stewards, councillors, trade union officials and journalists was setting off from Central Station, Glasgow, for London. Among the stewards there was even a newly wed who left his wife in the middle of their honeymoon to take part.

When they arrived at Euston at 6 a.m. the next morning, Benn was there to meet them.

That afternoon the stewards lobbied Westminster. A group of leading stewards along with Benn, Provost Robert Fleming of Clydebank, and the M.P.s for the areas concerned, met Heath at Downing Street. At first the Prime Minister had declined to see the delegation, letting it be known that he was willing to meet the S.T.U.C. delegation later in the week, but eventually they were let through a heavy police cordon to meet Heath, Sir John Eden, Minister for Industry, and Gordon Campbell. When they came in, Heath offered them tea, coffee or whisky. None took whisky.

After the meeting James Reid told the press, 'I got the impression we were talking to men who did not know what it means to stand in the dole queue or what it will mean to working class families - and worse who didn't appear to care'.

Later at the Commons the Scots went through the process of sending in 'Green Cards' for M.P.s they wished to lobby. Most were willing to come and hear the men's cause. Tam Galbraith, however, despite twenty-two green cards from constituents did not come out of the deep recesses of the Commons. But as he was leaving the Commons a group of U.C.S. workers saw him and surrounded him. Glasgow Herald writer, Charles Gillies, was there. He wrote the next day that Mr. Galbraith 'refused an invitation to go to Clydebank because he thought it would serve no useful purpose - adding that he might end up in the river.

'His visitors agreed that that might happen.'

On Monday 14 June, a group of women councillors picketted Lady Tweedsmuir, Minister of State for Scotland, when she went to open a health centre in Glasgow. Originally the opening had been timed for the afternoon but that morning it was suddenly moved forward to 10 a.m. It was the last public engagement in Glasgow by a minister till September.

The next day a group of churchmen of all denominations sent a telegram to Heath stating 'The dissolution of U.C.S. without the existence of

62

alternative industry would be so damaging to the
economy of Scotland and, in an area of already severe
unemployment, would have such social and economic
consequences as to be totally unacceptable in a
responsible society.

'We appeal to you beyond party controversy to
take action that this need not happen and to give firm
assurances now to this effect.' Heath refused to make
public the reply he sent when asked to do so later
that week by a Labour M.P.

On Friday of that week Gordon Campbell opened
the new airport hotel at Glasgow Airport outside the
city. He was met at the main entrance by about 100
U.C.S. men with banners. At first Mr. Campbell
declined a meeting with a delegation, but Norman
Buchan, the local M.P., persuaded him to agree to
a ten-minute meeting. The chief press officer at the
Scottish Office brusquely refused to allow a
photograph of the meeting.

That discussion was the first Campbell had with
either management or unions from U.C.S. since
November 1970.

Later the men and Mr. Buchan left to join a
further demonstration at Alexandria, a few miles
from Clydebank, where another factory, Plessey's,
was being closed with large redundancies. The
guests at the opening of the new hotel stayed behind
to hear speeches from Sir Charles Forte and Mr.
Campbell before tucking into salmon, and strawberries
and cream with champagne. Mr. Campbell was happy
to open the hotel and record his special pleasure in
the 225 jobs it was providing in an area of unemployment.
The jobs, naturally, were mostly suited to women and
not redundant shipyard workers.

That Sunday, prayers were said and petition forms
handed out in every Clydebank church. Sir Gerald
Nabarro, in a speech in Scotland, described the
stewards as 'silly billies' for wanting nationalisation
of the shipbuilding industry. On Monday the 21st, as
a delegation from the S.T.U.C. met Heath and
Davies, a meeting of over 700 shop stewards from
every major factory in the west of Scotland decided

Front line at June demo, l. to r.: Bob Cook (convener, Govan), James Airlie, Wedgwood Benn, Sam Barr, Bob Dickie, Willie McInnes (convener, Linthouse)

Platform at 18 August demo, l. to r.: Raymond Macdonald (chairman, S.T.U.C.), Robert Fleming (Provost, Clydebank), Wedgwood Benn, Dan McGarvey, Vic Feather, Hugh Scanlon, James Reid, William Ross, M.P.

to join the demonstration planned for the Wednesday by the U.C.S. stewards. Reid told the gathering at the Rosevale Bingo Hall in Partick, Glasgow: 'We have told the Government, "If you want us out of the yards let the Prime Minister and Davies come and try to do it." We don't only build boats on the Clyde, we build men who have guts and intelligence and who'll take some moving.'

On Wednesday the sun shone and history was made. Over 100,000 stopped work that afternoon. The demonstration of 40,000 marchers was the largest Clydeside protest since the General Strike. Three train loads of workers came from Clydebank; one train came from the Rolls Royce factory in Hillington; Chrysler, Singer, British Steel, Yarrow's - all joined the U.C.S. workers.

A group of 400 retired boilermakers came back early from their annual day trip to the Clyde Coast to join in. The whole city centre came to a halt as the marchers, sometimes twelve abreast, walked to Glasgow Green. The front line of Stewards and M.P.s linked arms in the style of the French working-class demonstrations. Wedgwood Benn and Scottish Communist Party executive member, James Reid, marching arm in arm was something new. The march filled the full width of Union Street in the city centre, a courtesy the police had never before extended - not even to the Orange Lodge.

As they marched in the sun, Gordon Campbell, the Secretary of State for Scotland, was 400 miles away in London telling M.P.s that the marchers 'would be better employed in their work, because leaving work is causing loss of industrial production in Scotland'.

Another 'Clyde' ship, the Samjohn Governor was launched the next day. The men watched as the shipyard manager at Clydebank, Mr. John Nicholls, pulled the switch without ceremony, then they went back to work. There was no cheering.

In July, the yards began closing for the summer holidays, Clydebank as a separate town from Glasgow had a different holiday period so, for four weeks, one or other of yards was unoccupied. Over twenty stewards did not go on holiday in order to be on hand to cope with the possibility that one or two of the yards might be closed and the men sacked while they were on holiday.

Through July the fight for U.C.S. took the normal form of previous redundancy fights. Petitions were collected, stewards addressed meetings around the country, delegations went to London. But all the time in the background there was the feeling that this was different, this was too big to be just another closure. The petition, for example, collected nearly 100,000 signatures within a few days of the forms being printed.

All the time, too, there was the knowledge that the men were planning for the takeover of the yards. The action to be taken was, by virtue of the uncertain future, naturally undefined. Neither the stewards nor anyone else could say what might happen. Newspaper speculation was forecasting the closure of Clydebank with the loss of 3,000 jobs.

The uncertainty, the 'Phoney War', resulted from the waiting for the report of the advisory committee.

VI

'CLYDE BUTCHERED'

It took Geddes fifty-three weeks, £56,313 and a 209-page report to create Upper Clyde Shipbuilders. It took the 'Four Wise Men' - as the advisory committee became known - six weeks and a three-page report to kill it.

Davies had announced in the 15 June debate in the Commons that three prominent businessmen had agreed to join his committee. The 'Three Wise Men' were Mr. Alexander McDonald, chairman of Distillers Company Ltd.; Sir Alexander Glen, chairman of Clarksons; and Mr. David Macdonald, a director of Hill Samuel, the merchant bankers.

As they neared the end of their inquiries Lord Robens, chairman of the National Coal Board joined as a fourth 'wise man'.

Davies told the stewards he met in Glasgow on 6 August that he had chosen the persons he did because he didn't want the committee to be experts in shipbuilding in case they were accused of bias as a result of their being competitors of Upper Clyde. They did however, said the Minister, have access to experts in shipbuilding. Who presumably, replied Reid, were direct competitors of U.C.S.

In any case, Davies' statement that these were not experts is a rather fine point. Two of the committee are very much involved in the world of ships. David Macdonald as well as being on the board of Hill Samuel - whose subsidiaries include the ship-owning firm Hill Samuel Insurance and Shipping Holdings Ltd. - is on the board of Austin and Pickersgill, the Wearside shipbuilders, of which Kenneth Douglas had been Managing Director. (Hill Samuel, incidentally, was the fourth largest contributor - along with Stenhouse Holdings - to the Conservative Party in 1969.)

Sir Alexander Glen, too, has large shipping interests. He is deputy chairman of Shipping Industrial Holdings Ltd. and chairman of its subsidiary Clarksons. He moved up to deputy chairman on the resignation in June 1970 of Reginald Maudling to become Home Secretary.

S.I.H. is a vast holding company which wholly or partly controls over 180 companies. These range from Trident Insurance Co. Ltd., the Clarkson Holidays group of companies, to smaller firms like Bad Debt Protection Ltd. On the shipping side it includes Scotscraig Shipping Co. Ltd., Scotstoun Shipping Co. Ltd., Dene Shipping Co. Ltd. and many other shipping firms. Clarksons are the main brokers for the Scott-Lithgow group on Lower Clyde.

When the group was formed, Gordon Campbell said that it contained 'three leading Scots whose main concern must be the welfare of Scotland and Clydeside'.

Sir Alexander Glen's companies at the date of liquidation had eight ships on order. One was with Scott-Lithgow. Two were with Sumitomo Shipbuilding and Machinery Co. Ltd.; three with Mitsubishi Heavy Industries Ltd.; and two with Nippon Kokan Kabushiki Kaisha - all of Japan.

In his annual report Sir Alexander noted: 'Our entire shipbuilding programme is on a fixed price basis and at a level which appears increasingly favourable.' The two orders from Nippon Kokan had been placed in Japan, he said, where they would be eligible 'for investment grants and are at fixed prices, financed by long-term loans from Japan at low fixed rates of interest'.

These Government aids from Japan plus more direct subsidies given to the Japanese shipbuilders enabled Clarksons shipowning and shipbroking divisions to notch up a 1970 profit of £1,723,000. That figure does not include the projected £1,100,000 expected to accrue from the merger with the Dene group of companies.

Yet nowhere in the advisory committee report is a mention made of investment grants, subsidies or other forms of Government aid to shipbuilding. These would of course be paid for by the British and not the Japanese taxpayer.

Despite these massive profits - the S.I.H. total profit was £4,247,215 - Sir Alexander's companies only managed to give £546 to Conservative Party funds.

The third 'wise man' was **Alexander** Forbes **McDonald** whose company, D.C.L. manufactures most of the big selling whiskies and gins - including Haigs, Johnny Walker, and Gordons and Booths gins. He is also a director of the National and Commercial Banking Group Ltd.

A minor point made by the committee in its report was that wages at U.C.S. had been too high and would have to become more 'competitive'. Mr. McDonald earns £661.50 a week.

The fourth member was Lord Robens, the late Alf, who had been Labour M.P. for Blyth before becoming the chairman of the National Coal Board. Over the years he has acquired directorships in the Bank of England; British Fuel Co. Ltd.; J.H. Sankey and son; Johnson, Mathey and Co. Ltd.; Times Newspapers Ltd. He is also a director of Vickers Ltd., who gave £5,202 to anti-socialist political organisations.* His appointment was announced on 24 June.

A few weeks after the report of the 'Four Wise Men' was issued Lord Robens revealed to an English T.V. reporter that he no longer considered himself a socialist. Jimmy Reid commented: 'That's like the

---

*In 1969 before the election, £2,500 to British United Industrialists, £1,000 to Economic League and £1,702 to Common Cause. The last is less anti-socialist than the others but is nevertheless a political organisation under the terms of the act.

Rev. Ian Paisley calling a press conference to announce he's not a Catholic. '

The committee of three met the shop stewards at the beginning of their inquiry and parted amicably, the stewards feeling they had had a sympathetic hearing. They felt that the committee had promised to take social considerations into account, as did other community leaders and M.P.s who met them. Sir Donald Liddle, Glasgow's Lord Provost said after meeting them: 'We gather they are extremely keen indeed to find a viable proposition for shipbuilding on the Upper Clyde. ' Former Scottish Secretary William Ross said: 'I am certain that they have not been brought to recommend a brutal, butchering job. I am pretty hopeful that there will be continued shipbuilding on the Clyde'. ('It just shows how wrong you can be, ' grumbled Ross later).

Bruce Millan, M.P. said: 'I am willing to accept that they have an understanding of the human and social consequences for Clydeside'.

In the meantime the Government were keeping the yards going at great cost. Mr. Smith had been given permission by the Scottish courts to raise a loan from the Government to meet his needs. On 23 June the B.S.C. began supplying steel to the consortium again after receiving a guarantee that all supplies would be paid for. A better financial deal for future sales of steel was also agreed.

The liquidator required about £500,000 for each week's bills. Wages alone cost £250,000. The Government gave him £3 million to cover costs till 6 August.

Ridley went to some pains in the Commons to stress that the money would be recovered from future deliveries and was therefore in its effect a short term loan from the Government.

First hint of trouble ahead came on 27 July when word got out that the final report of the committee had been given to John Davies. An official from his department was in permanent attendance on the committee during its investigations and the Minister knew, before he received it, what was coming.

The stewards tried all day unsuccessfully to contact the committee, claiming that they had been promised another meeting before any recommendation was finalised. Reid said: 'We were given a pledge that they would meet us again. They had time to see any industrialist who wanted their name in the papers but not apparently the men whose livelihood depends on their recommendations.'

They went down to London on the 27th and sat in on a late night debate on unemployment in Scotland. To those who had never been in the House before it was a great shock to see only six or seven M.P.s on the Government benches and about three times that number opposite.

They sat in silent anger in the gallery as Scots Tory back-bencher Jock Bruce-Gardyne, Gordon Campbell's P.P.S. and M.P. for South Angus and Mearns launched an attack on themselves. He asked Nicholas Ridley, who was winding up for the Government, if it was a fact that 'there are elements among the trade unions on the Upper Clyde who have indicated to any present employees of U.C.S. that if they should consider applying for jobs with Yarrow's or with Lower Clyde they would do so at risk to their families?'

In the face of opposition anger he continued: 'These reports are circulating.' Benn accused him of repeating 'filthy tittle tattle', Norman Buchan M.P. described it as 'frivolity, callousness and smears' and warned that if the yards were not kept intact the Government would face the kind of anger 'which this class-ridden Government cannot conceive.'

'The Government have made the class struggle respectable.'

The Cabinet met a day early on Wednesday 28 July and discussed the report for the 'Four Wise Men'. At question time on the Thursday the benches were packed to hear Davies' statement. The afternoon papers were still talking about 2,000 to 3,000 redundancies.

As the normal question time progressed the front bench spokesmen dropped out of the chamber for a few minutes to collect the first copies of the report from the Vote Office. When they returned William Ross glowered up to the public gallery, where the stewards sat, and shook his head grimly.

The torpedo was primed.

Minutes later it left a bloody big hole in the side of Upper Clyde Shipbuilders. The Minister told the packed chamber that the Government had decided to close both the Clydebank and Scotstoun yards in light of the advisory committee's report.

Their conclusion had been, he said, that the company had been doomed from the start as a result of the faulty concept of structure, the heavy inherited losses, and bad management. The report also stated that the order book for the company had been dangerously thin.

Nevertheless, said Davies, if the orders were concentrated at Govan and Linthouse; if management was radically reformed; and if 'more productive and realistic' working arrangements and wage rates were negotiated, a new company could be set up to continue shipbuilding on the upper reaches.

Given all these circumstances the jobs of 2,500 workers could be saved.

As the house sat in silence the quiet voice of a Scots Labour M.P. drifted across the stunned benches saying 'God Almighty!'

By the time the statement had been finished, the benches were seething. On the Opposition side dozens of members were on their feet shouting 'Resign'. On the Government side many were standing cheering and taunting the other side. Most political commentators compared the scene with the Suez debate in 1956.

Gordon Campbell of the Scottish Daily Express wrote:

Not since the sensational scenes over the Suez invasion has Tory government faced such wrath. The suntanned Mr. Heath, flanking Mr. Davies and Scottish Secretary Gordon Campbell on the Government Front Bench, stared balefully around him as outraged Labour M.P.s heaped screaming abuse on his head.

Benn was finally able to get his questions in. He pointed out that as well as losing two yards this meant a direct loss of jobs for 6,000 people as well as a possible 15,000 people employed in ancillary industries, and added: 'This is a major tragedy for the men involved and for Scotland, and it has been introduced by the Right Hon. Gentleman without a single word of regret at any state in his statement'.

A raging Ross roared 'Resign' again and again at Davies. He shouted: 'This is not a re-construction; it is butchery.' The Speaker had to call the House to order repeatedly. Wilson began to say, 'In view of the callous and unfeeling attitude of the Secretary Of State...' but was drowned out by jeers and shouts from the Conservative back-benchers.

Benn finally succeeded in proposing a motion for an adjournment debate on U.C.S. When the Speaker asked those who wanted a debate to stand, the Opposition was again roused to fury when not one Tory M.P. stood to call for a debate.

The time of the debate was set for the following Monday but the stewards in the gallery had other ideas about the next battle ground. They flew back to Glasgow for a mass meeting the following morning.

The report of the 'Four Wise Men' was published only in shortened form and contained no information on who was seen or what evidence was examined by the committee. While they did not see Anthony Wedgwood Benn, who had been the Minister responsible for setting up the company they felt able to say that it had a 'totally mistaken initial structure'.

They pointed out that the contracts which U.C.S. had inherited from the old companies on formation had been estimated at the time would cost U.C.S. £3.55 million. In the long run these inherited costs came to £12 million. Other orders had been taken on at the beginning at an estimated loss of £4.8 million. In fact they had cost £9.8 million.

It accused poor management of not exercising efficient control of costs, especially wages, which threatened other industries on the Clyde because of their size.

It concluded that, 'Any continuation of Upper Clyde Shipbuilders in its present form would be wholly unjustified and, indeed, could cause serious and more widespread damage'. Accordingly it recommended the measures taken by Davies.

Justifying its findings the report said: 'In these recommendations we have tried to make judgments primarily on grounds of likely commercial viability both in a short and longer term sense, but, in view of Government's share of responsibility, we have also given weight to social considerations which we believe Government in this case must observe.'

In recommending that the order book be based on Govan yard allied with the steel fabrication facilities of Linthouse the report stated: 'We should also mention that there is considerable misunderstanding about this present programme. Looked at in total it may seem large, but spread as it was over the three U.C.S. yards it was already dangerously thin in the light of the present depressed conditions in world shipping.'

Redundant staff and workers could, it said, be employed at Lower Clyde, Yarrow's and elsewhere. Work already underway should be completed.

To achieve acceptable productivity at the new yard there would have to be double shift working. This and the other proposals would have to be conditional on:

1. The full co-operation of the unions in making this venture succeed. In particular the acceptance of double shift working and 'competitive wage rates'.

2. Adequate capital being forthcoming.

3. Satisfactory management.

The four advisers recognised that financial support from suppliers would be difficult to obtain and would need a degree of Government involvement, which might at the start mean the Government bearing the total financial burden or at least providing guarantees.

There was a universally shocked reaction to the announcement. Clydebank's provost Robert Fleming said: 'We are absolutely shattered. The worst has happened. If the men barricade themselves in the yards and behave with dignity they will get public sympathy and support from everyone.

'Many local shopkeepers will be forced to close. This will be a progressive thing, a form of local economic cancer.'

A.U.E.W. organiser in Glasgow Mr. John Sheriff added: 'I have never encountered a more soul-less Government. This is the kind of action which created the I.R.A. in Ireland.'

Dismay was expressed by all sides of industry in Scotland. A statement from the Scottish Council (Development and Industry) said: 'By any calculation it is a black day for the Clyde and for Scotland.' A Scottish spokesman for the C.B.I. said: 'It is a pretty black picture...a very disappointing result to have redundancies to this extent. The unemployment position in the west of Scotland is so bad that anything that adds to it can only be looked at with alarm.'

The Daily Record ran a front page editorial entitled, 'Clyde Butchered'. Even Charles Graham, the emotional Daily Express leader writer in Scotland had to say: 'The blackest pessimist could not have foreseen the butchery that would be perpetrated by this Government upon the shipyard workers of the Upper Clyde.'

Of Davies he said: 'John Davies is the man who is being tongue-lashed from all sides. Partly because he is the prime bearer of the bad news. Partly because of the manner of his bearing it. He is provocative to an incredible degree'.

Mr. Graham counselled against any take-over, though, by the U.C.S. workers. That would he said only 'win a few days publicity that will avail them nothing and that will pay dividends only in the pages of Pravda and the councils of the Kremlin'.

The stewards, naturally, had a few words to say about the report and the statement. James Airlie said: 'Defeat is unthinkable, but if we are defeated we will have turned the whole of Scotland upside down. It's our birthright to work on the Clyde and we mean to work there. '

James Reid said: 'Men from Mars would have more sympathy with the lives of ordinary people. The cannibalistic brutality of this Government is unbelievable. They have got a fight on their hands such as no amateur yachtsman could ever have conceived. '

Gerry Ross, who had been left in charge at Clyde-bank, received a phone call to tell him the bad news. He turned to the waiting reporters and said dogmatically: 'It will be over our dead bodies. We would be better dying in the yard fighting than starving into submission on the dole queue. '

Stewards had already been assigned to gate duty at the four divisions though only Clydebank was working that week. The Glasgow yards were still on their annual Fair holiday. The gatemen still carried out their duties but the stewards kept a watching brief.

In the early sixties when Denny's yard in Dumbarton faced bankruptcy, the men left work as usual on Friday evening. Over the weekend the closure was announced and the gates were padlocked when the men returned on Monday morning.

The memory of that was a long time dying.

VII

'LAME DUCKS AND WEEKEND DRAKES'

The Prime Minister's face was like thunder as he
jumped down onto the pier from Morning Cloud, his
yacht. He was annoyed and he didn't try to hide it. A
bright sun was shining down on Cowes but Mr. Heath's
face did not reflect it.

As a result of heavy newspaper pressure, the
premier had been forced to give up his sailing on
Monday 2 August to go back to the House of Commons.
It meant that he, as captain of the British team, had
to miss a race in the Admiral's Cup series. On the
Thursday before, Mr. Heath had been heard to shout
'shut up' at Wilson during the general melee after the
announcement by John Davies. What caused his
outburst is not certain though many reporters claimed
that Wilson had been taunting the P.M. over his plans
to be sailing during the Monday emergency debate.
Wilson has since denied this.

Yachting is not one of the great British spectator
sports. Nor, in fact, has it been noted as a very
successful participatory sport for the British in
recent years. The British victory in the Admiral's
Cup - the high spot of our racing calendar - should
have been a tremendous publicity coup for the Prime
Minister.

Only three years before, Mr. Heath had been sailing
dinghies. Now he was about to become a victorious
British captain and he patently didn't want to miss any
of the fun.

A full colour page in the Daily Express appeared as
part of the build up to his victory. It showed a tanned

premier on his yacht, <u>Morning Cloud</u>*. The copy read 'A yard won or lost usually makes the difference between victory and defeat'. Now in the middle of the series of races by ocean-going yachts the four yards of Upper Clyde were winning and the P.M. boarded an R.A.F. helicopter, which was waiting at Cowes to fly him to Chequers.

As the 'chopper' rose up against the sun, the stewards were leaving their first co-ordinating committee since the yards had been taken over on the Friday 30 July. They had decided that they could not wait for the predictable result of the Commons debate, and the yards were in their control.

The men had seized the initiative from the Government and they were still uncertain what to do with it. Every steward, indeed every Left-winger on Clydeside, had their pet schemes for asserting the takeover. So much so that every Sunday newspaper had been able to lead off with a different angle on the situation.

<u>The People</u> had the stewards organising a bonfire for the several thousand liquidation notices sent to the men. The <u>Daily Mirror</u>, from somewhere, discovered a £10 million appeal for the stewards' fighting fund. The Scottish papers discussed a proposal that Glasgow and neighbouring local authorities should take over the yards and run them as a municipal concern.

What appeared to be the most fanciful of these stories was actually the closest to fact. <u>The Sunday Times</u> revealed that the committee had decided to take the keel of ship 121, a product carrier ordered by the Haverton line, from Linthouse, where it was lying in fifty-ton pre-assembly units.

The ship had originally been scheduled for completion at Scotstoun but now that the yard was threatened with closure it was feared it would be

---

*The yacht will always be known on Clydeside as <u>Mourning Clyde</u> - a title which appeared on numerous posters and banners.

transferred to Govan instead. Plans were made to load the units onto a barge and float them across the river to Scotstoun.

To precipitate a decision the Scotstoun convener put his men who were 'working in' at the end of August onto work preparing the steel panelling prior to the arrival of the units from Linthouse. The committee went to the liquidator and told him that if he did not order the keel over they would take it themselves. It was floated over forty-eight hours later. But on 1 August the stewards angrily denied that this was their intention.

Taking advantage of the fine weather, a group of waiting journalists stood around in the middle of the vast yard carpark chatting. The yards were still and the only activity was in the joinery shop where thirty men were working overtime on a special contract for Cammell Laird's shipyard.

Waiting with them were two nice young kids from the Glasgow Claimants and Unemployed Workers Union. They had come to offer to help the shipyard workers with their 'social security problems'. Their offer - genuinely made - only raised a smile in the physical surrounds of acres of empty shipyard. Nobody was unkind enough to suggest that if the state couldn't cope with the problem it was going to take more than the enthusiasm of two students. As they waited they discussed the OZ trial and their own forthcoming legal proceedings for selling the Little Red Schoolbook in Glasgow.

They were the first of many representatives of left-wing groups from Britain and the continent to visit the new Mecca of the Left. After the takeover, a larger selection of socialist and Marxist newspapers were sold at the gates each lunchtime than W.H. Smith has ever refused to distribute.

The stewards came out to meet the reporters in the middle of the Clydebank carpark. Airlie began by appealing to the Labour movement for financial support. He said: 'We can only be beaten if we are starved into submission'. It was a phrase like 'The Right to Work' that became identified with the campaign.

Reid condemned the announcement by the liquidator that the first redundancies would fall in the marketing and forward planning departments. He said angrily: 'The report ('Four Wise Men') says that the order book is too thin. Then they sack the people who can rectify this situation, which, in any case, we have explained was a deliberate policy.

'If they do that then we will send our own 'Marketeers' abroad to secure orders.' This did not, he added with a grin, imply support for the Common Market.

The day before, Saturday 31 July, someone had blown up John Davies' flat. He was in his Knutsford home at the time and was not involved in the blast. He returned to London to inspect the damage. He told newsmen that it had caused a lot of damage, but fortunately had missed his wine cellar. He added that the bomb had obvious connections 'with political developments over the past weeks involving Upper Clyde Shipbuilders.'

He joined Heath and Scottish Secretary Gordon Campbell at Chequers on Sunday evening, where it was decided he should go to Glasgow. It was obvious that the Opposition would press strongly the point that no Minister had visited the area or the yards.

When the Commons assembled on Monday 2 August there were, for the first time, no stewards in the gallery. Their centre of power had moved northwards. Since the motion had been placed by the Labour opposition, Anthony Wedgwood Benn was the opening speaker and, in common with all his major speeches on the subject, he went into a long detailed defence of his own part in the creation of the company. He conceded that, as the 'Four Wise Men' had said, there were faults in creation. He said: 'Looking back over the years of U.C.S. and with the benefit of hindsight, I have no doubt in my mind that it would have been better if the previous Government had taken the whole industry into public ownership at the time we launched our programme. We should have re-equipped and rationalised and swept aside the old owners.'

80

He accused the Government of a prior desire to destroy the company, of misleading the House on their intentions and thereby of wasting a priceless asset, the skill of the people who work at U.C.S. He ended: 'In the process they are deliberately sentencing thousands of people to a slow and living death of long-term unemployment in the wasteland of west central Scotland which the Government has decided to create.

'The Prime Minister's epitaph will be: "He is the man who forgot the people", and the people will never forgive him for it. '

The accusation that the Government had shown no feeling for the men and their plight was beginning to irk Davies. He began his reply by saying he would like to refer to a matter that was distressing him greatly. 'It is that in any sense I personally have lacked sympathy for the situation which has arisen. Anybody who knows me will readily recognise how unlikely that is. '

It was a transformation from his previous Commons speech on the subject and the sharp eye of Norman Shrapnel of <u>The Guardian</u> saw it more clearly than anyone. He wrote the next day:

> Having failed last week to say a word of sympathy for the men's plight, Mr. Davies was now so full of regrets and anxious feelings on their behalf, he might have been spending sleepless nights thinking of them. He was greatly distressed at what he called, 'this dreadful disaster'. He deeply sympathised. He deplored it all as much as anybody. The impact was going to be very grave indeed. All the same...the best thing to do now was to follow the 'sensible and practical advice' of the advisory group.

Understandably much of the debate centred on the effects closure would have on Clydebank. Glasgow Labour M.P. Bruce Millan said: 'We have a report which dismisses Clydebank in half a sentence. A town cannot be condemned to death in half a sentence in a three-page report. '

William Ross was still angry from the Thursday announcement when he had been in a roaring rage at the Tory front bench. He explained the feelings that caused his outburst: 'I spoke angrily about Clydebank, but the Rt. Hon. Gentleman should appreciate that the people who died in the Clydebank Blitz (in which several hundred people were killed in one night in 1941) died for John Brown's. The enemy was not aiming at people, but at John Brown's and the one place that was not touched was John Brown's, but the Government are going to kill it.'

The number of Scots Tories taking part in the debate was twice the total for the 15 June debate. Galbraith and Campbell were joined by Edward Taylor and Ian MacArthur, M.P. for Perth and East Perthshire. Neither the latter nor his speech had much relevance to shipbuilding or Clydeside.

The former, however, departed slightly from the united front put up by his colleagues. Ministerial responsibility had barred him from previous debates, but he had now become the first Tory to resign from the Heath Government. He had left over his opposition to the Common Market but it was well known he was also unhappy about the Upper Clyde decisions.

During the 15 June debate he had been forced to sit in agonised silence as Benn and Ross produced quotes made by him, during the 1969 crisis, demanding more money for the company. As he sat sadly on the Government front bench he had raised his head occasionally to nod in agreement with his words of 1969.

While the Government should not be blamed for the situation, said Mr. Taylor, those who blamed it on the work force were being equally unfair. 'I have seen the men who work there, and the report we have received proves beyond a shadow of a doubt that even if every man working in the Upper Clyde was an industrial angel and if they had worked seven days a week, without a day off, and without striking, the yards, in their present situation, could not have paid. It is wrong to allocate the entire responsibility to the men.'

And he rebuked his colleagues who said, 'Why not have one union instead of hundreds?' 'They fail to realise,' said Mr. Taylor, 'that in recent years in most shipyards, not only in the Clyde but all over Britain, the platers, the caulkers, welders, drillers, and the shipwrights have all come together in one union, and demarcation problems have ceased to exist. Terrific progress has been made in this direction.'

It was not what could be termed an attack on the Government, but set next to the views of hard liners like Galbraith and Ridley it was a definite deviation from the closed ranks of the laisser-faire mob. What made it all the more unusual was that Taylor is a leading acolyte of Enoch Powell, the Adam Smith of Wolverhampton.

But Mr. Taylor has unusual circumstances. His majority comes from a huge working class council house scheme in Glasgow. Many of his voters work in shipbuilding or the ancillary industries. In any case he himself is more working class than other Tory M.P.s

He tells, against himself, the story of being approached in the Commons cafetera by a senior Conservative to ask for a pair. His approach to politics is essentially populist and there are a lot of people in Clydeside.

Mr. Heath did not take part in the debate he had been so unwilling to attend and sat with a bored expression through the opening and closing speeches. At one point as he sat with his hand shading his eyes a Labour backbencher shouted: 'Why doesn't someone wake up Ted?'

William Ross, who was speaking at the time, replied with unusual wit: 'It's too late to wake him up. The Government are playing ducks and drakes with the Scottish economy - they are lame ducks and weekend Drakes.'

After the debate ended with the expected Conservative majority, the Prime Minister flew back to Cowes to beat the American Armada.

Police outrider being asked to leave by Reid
Harold Wilson in the Clydebank canteen

VIII

'I JUST DON'T UNDERSTAND YOU'

When John Davies had told the Commons he was
going to Glasgow, he was warned by Clydebank M.P.
Hugh McCartney to take a good bodyguard. He did.

When the plane landed at Abbotsinch airport
outside Glasgow there were police everywhere. They
were stationed at every door, on the terminal roof
and at the Minister's side. He brought two armed
bodyguards with him and other detectives from
Glasgow's Special Branch shadowed him at all times.
Dog handlers guarded his plane till he flew back
again that evening. At the City Chambers in Glasgow
he was met by about 100 placard-carrying
demonstrators...and fifty policemen.

All pressmen had to show their cards to get in. All,
that is, except a representative of the Economist who
parked his car at the back and walked in through a
side entrance. He was at the press conference before
he saw a policeman.

Glasgow's Lord Provost had been asked to invite a
representative cross section of Clydeside industry to
discuss the situation. There was Hamish Grant,
Scottish secretary of the C.B.I.; Robin MacLellan, of
Glasgow Chamber of Commerce; conveners of the
main counties in west Scotland; councillors from
Glasgow and Clydebank.

The workers' side was well represented with
James Jack and Raymond MacDonald, the General
Secretary and chairman of the S.T.U.C.; Joe Black
and James Ramsay of the 'Confed.', both of whom had
been on continual attendance at U.C.S. for weeks. The
stewards were represented by Bob Dickie and Sam

Barr, the conveners of the two doomed yards. James Reid attended in his capacity as a Clydebank councillor.

The meeting began in the Glasgow Corporation chamber at 11 a.m. The Provost chaired the meeting and Davies and Campbell sat on the raised dais beside him looking down on the mahogany and red leather benches. They began by emphasising that they had not come to offer any new formula or action. What they wanted was ideas to come from the floor. For several hours - with a lunch break - the arguments flew across the room with even the C.B.I. representative delivering a mild rebuke to his former boss.

Eventually just before 5 p.m. Joe Black stood up and said he saw no point in going on with a one-sided dialogue and if no progress was to be offered he was leaving. The stewards, union officials and the Clydebank councillors left too. In a neighbouring room they held a press conference to explain their walkout, (the talks had been in private).

As they left their press conference Davies and the others who had remained behind, left the council chamber. The two groups encountered each other in the corridor and in front of the reporters and photographers an amazing scene developed. It personalised and symbolised the huge gulf between the workers of Upper Clyde and the Government.

As Davies walked past he pushed out a hand to Jimmy Reid. As Reid explained to the stewards meeting the next day, when someone comes towards you with his hand out your instinctive reaction is to put yours out. The steward caught himself in time and placed his hand on the Minister's shoulder instead, and said: 'I cannot shake hands with you. I cannot possibly shake hands with you.' Davies said something about shaking hands as friends, but Reid persisted: 'You are no friend of mine, I cannot possibly shake hands with you.'

By now everyone was watching and listening and flashlights were sparking off all around. Davies, trying to recoup the situation, said: 'I would like to shake hands with you not as a friend, but as one fighting for a common cause.' An amazed Reid snapped back: 'Don't you know that shipbuilding on the upper reaches of the Clyde is the best in the world? Let's try to keep it that way.'

Davies had one final try. 'I have found interest in what you have been saying today. We must work in a concerted effort to see the future clearly.' But as they moved away Davies said: 'I just don't understand you' and Reid left with the same words, 'And I don't understand you'.

The Minister left Glasgow with a large sheaf of notes he and Campbell had taken, which he promised to study. At length.

The stewards had let it be known that they were willing to invite Davies to the yard at Clydebank, but they would not allow his large bodyguard in with him. Airlie told reporters that the men would extend the 'usual Clydeside courtesy - and I don't mean we'll chuck him in the river.'

But if John Davies showed no inclination to go to Clydebank and do the Grand Tour there were plenty of others queuing up to. Each morning of the first weeks over eighty reporters, photographers and film crews crammed into the tiny smoke-filled classroom to attend the daily press conference.

In fact so many cameras were stationed about the place that the yard, with its long high-roofed sheds began to look, even more than usual, like a Hollywood film lot. The B.B.C. had four crews alone. One for colour news, one for black and white news, one documentary and one religious broadcasting. And they accused shipbuilding of overmanning!

There was a Swedish unit - 'Mr. Davies speaks Swedish, you know' - and at least two American ones. They were very happy to be in Scotland. A Californian cameraman told me, 'I always like coming to Britain, but it was getting to be a bit much. We've been in Belfast twenty-three times in the past two years.' They were all there the day Harold Wilson came to visit.

He was not the first party leader to identify with the U.C.S. campaign. On the day Davies was in

Glasgow both Billy Wolfe of the Scottish National Party and John Gollan of the Communist Party paid their respects. The support of these parties, especially in money, was important, but the arrival of the leader of the Labour Party was of political importance.

It was all very well for Wedgwood Benn to talk about the birth of industrial democracy, the stuff of which great events are made, the power of the workers not going to be snuffed out etc. for he was a well-known advocate of workers' participation and openly admitted that he hoped that the U.C.S. fight would lead to the adoption by the Labour Party of his views. But it would be a great advance for the Left if the Labour Party was to support a stewards-led group of men in a course of action which could easily have involved illegal action. If the Labour Party was to support it, then Wilson would be the man who would have to commit the party.

Benn knew this and persuaded the former Labour Prime Minister to go to Scotland. Wilson was willing, but emphasised that he was going to hear the views of all the parties interested including the management and especially the S.T.U.C.

Mr. Wilson arrived at the yard gates on Wednesday 4 August, and like everyone else was stopped by the stewards. It was a formality in his case, but they were unwilling to admit some of his company. His car had been preceded by two police outriders on his drive from Glasgow and they were asked to leave by Reid, who told them, 'There are no hooligans in this yard.'

For Wilson the visit must have brought back pleasant memories. There had not been many chances in the previous twelve months to repeat his election 'meet the people' walkabouts. Here he was overwhelmed with people to meet. Both in the yard and on a 200-yard walk to Clydebank Town Hall for lunch, he was cheered by the U.C.S. men and their families. Clydebank is a stronghold of the Left- but it doesn't get many visits from its political leaders.

The Leader of the Opposition was swept round the yard at breakneck speed in a large crowd of stewards,

journalists and curious workers. Airlie had told
Wilson he was in no need of protection and was among
friends in the yards. That was true of the workers,
but when Wilson entered the vast canteen he was in
grave danger of being swamped by pressmen.

If he was going to give Labour Party support to the
'work-in' this was where he would do it and nobody
wanted to miss it. The workers were sitting at the
long rows of tables eating their lunch of stew and
potatoes. Wilson spoke without a microphone, standing
on a bench with the press milling about him, in a
great plate-breaking, stew-swilling mob.

He said: 'This is not the first time I have been to
Clydebank but I never expected to come here for such
a situation as you are facing today. There are just
three things I want to say to you.

'First I am here to express on behalf of the whole
British Labour movement our support for Upper Clyde
shipbuilding workers in what they are facing at this
time.' Secondly, he said, he wanted to get all the
facts he could before making a statement and would
be meeting the S.T.U.C., the provosts of Glasgow
and Clydebank and Ken Douglas as well as the
stewards.

'But the third and final thing I want to say to you is
this. That on behalf of the British Labour movement
I am here to assert the right of the shipbuilding
workers of Upper Clyde - the right to work.' The men
cheered and banged the tables.

They had interpreted his words as meaning support
for the 'work-in' but they are capable of being under-
stood differently. He had not, as some papers said
the next day, said he supported the men in what they
were 'doing', but in what they were 'facing'.

He was questioned after his press conference in
Glasgow on the exact meaning of his words. He told
News at Ten reporter Martyn Lewis: 'I said that we,
the whole Labour movement, asserted their right to
work, which is a human democratic right. So far as
the 'work-in' is concerned I said don't let anybody
condemn them, who is not facing these anxieties -
provided they act within the law.'

Lewis: 'So in terms of the action they are taking now you would support the 'work-in' so long as they stay within the law?'

Wilson: 'I think it's a natural reaction. I think it's a hopeless reaction.'

He corrected himself: 'It comes out of hopelessness and anxiety. No, what I support is a scheme which makes these things unnecessary.'

Whether or not Wilson gave his party's support to the 'work-in' became academic as he returned to London to call a special midnight meeting of Scots Labour M.P.s to report on his visit and to tell them he had never been so affected by a situation since Aberfan. It was taken by most commentators that the Labour Party was now backing the stewards.

Nobody present at the standing ovation given to the stewards at the Labour Party Conference in Brighton in October could have doubted that the rank and file of the party were 100 per cent behind the 'work-in'. The spontaneous demonstration was unparalleled in the party's history. But then so much of the support given to the men was without precedent.

With that visit by Wilson, the defences were complete. The militant stewards of Upper Clyde - many of them Communists - were now leading and acting as the spokesmen for the whole Labour movement.

Including John and Yoko, who sent £1,000 and a dozen roses.

IX

THERE MUST BE ANOTHER WAY

Nobody was surprised to learn that Wilson disagreed
with both the findings and the solution of the 'Four
Wise Men'. There were few people in Britain who did
not either directly, or by implication, feel that there
was another answer to the U.C.S. problem.

Among the thousands of letters received by the
stewards, were many offering advice or help. One
inventor wrote to tell them of his detailed plans for a
ship design including removeable engines. Then when
they were torpedoed, the salvaged engines could be
put in other vessels.

A Hong Kong shipping broker offered to find orders
for the workers while he was on a four-week world
tour. A few weeks before he had made headlines by
successfully penetrating the Number Ten Downing
Street security by posing as a waiter at a dinner
party given by Ted Heath.

A Scots immigrant in Australia, now retired, said
he could raise £10 million from people he had
encountered while working there as a clerk in the civil
service. He had been a bricklayer in John Brown's
after the war.

They at least were optimistic. It is known that
several Scots industrialists, including Lord Weir,
turned down offers to become chairman of Govan
Shipbuilders Ltd. before party-stalward Hugh
Stenhouse accepted. Their reasons are private, but
they too were expressing, by their refusal, little
confidence in the findings of the advisory committee.

The management of the company naturally
disagreed with the whole proceeding. They had, after

all, asked for money to keep the company going in its present form because they believed it was finally heading out of the red. Douglas has claimed that in the year ending August 1972 a profit of about £3½ million would have been reached. Certainly the trend of the losses was in that direction. In the first year, 1968, the company lost £9½ million; in 1969 they lost £12.1 million; from August 1969 to August 1970 the loss was down to £4.1 million; the projected loss for August 1970-71 was just over £3 million.

The Shipbuilding Industry Board, too, felt that good times were at long last ahead. In their report for the year ending March 1971 the board said: 'With the end of loss-making orders, more settled industrial relations and improved production, the company should make the long-awaited turn to profitability.'

The solutions offered ranged from selling off the assets to Lower Clyde and others, à la Ridley, to complete nationalisation as suggested in Benn's belated U.C.S. (Public Ownership) Bill published on 22 June 1971. Between these two positions were many alternatives...

Harold Wilson's answer was a form of Government takeover. The state, he argued, should take over the financial responsibility for the company for 'a long enough period'. A proposal had been discussed for running the two doomed yards down over a five-year period. Wilson said at his Glasgow press conference on 4 August that the length of period of Government responsibility for seeing the company out of the present situation should not be fixed. 'There should be an adequate period of years for U.C.S. to show what they can do.'

In a statement in the Commons the next day, he amplified his plan. 'One might be wrong. At the end of the day one might find that it could not become viable and that it is being squeezed, it is being strangled, because of the financial grip rather than because of any regard to the efficiency of the yards.' If that happened then the Government should put up the money to see through reforms of organisation, including workers' participation.

In addition, Mr. Wilson proposed a new company policy to deal with the cash flow situation which was mainly affected by the cyclical nature of the ordering and building of ships. He suggested building ships 'on spec'. The government could order six each of the three types of standardised ship U.C.S. had designed, the Clyde, the Super Clyde, and a multi-purpose bulk carrier.

The orders for these pre-production ships would be agreed between the Government and the company at a fair competitive price. 'If there is an active demand for ships the Government will make a profit. If there is a state of continued depression the ships may have to be stored for a little while or sold for less than the Government paid. '

There are precedents for Governments placing pre-production orders. The Labour Government did it during a slump in the machine tool industry. Both Labour and Conservatives used the technique to help the computer industry. As Mr. Wilson pointed out, advance factories - a policy supported by all parties - are a form of pre-production order.

In shipbuilding too there are examples of yard owners taking up slack during depressed ordering times by starting ships without a definite owner in sight. Sir William Lithgow's father kept his yards on Lower Clyde going before the war by adopting the system.

The plan for running down the two yards over a phased period had been put to Mr. Davies during his 6 August visit by management consultant J.H.F. Macmichael.

Macmichael is a director of the P-E Consulting Group and had been a member with Hepper of the working party set up by the S.I.B. in 1967 to organise the creation of U.C.S. He had also been retained by the company during the summer crisis of 1969 to draw up a plan for the re-construction of the company to meet the requirements being laid down by Benn before he would increase the Government loan. Part of his proposals then had been for a five-year period in which the company and its deliveries would be guaranteed by the Government in order to create supplier confidence. Benn refused to give such a guarantee.

He attended the City Chambers meeting with Davies as a representative of Glasgow Chamber of Commerce, though his proposal was a personal idea. Briefly his plan was to create a new company based on the Scotstoun and Clydebank yards which would be run down over a five-year period. In this time a phased programme of retraining and redeployment would be carried out with 600 men leaving every six months either through natural wastage or to go to other work found by Government agencies.

In an article in the Glasgow Herald explaining his plan, he pointed out that the most conservative estimate of the possible redundancies in ancillary trades was 6,000, which meant that at a minimum, on the current rates, the Government was faced with a bill of £50 million in order to find new jobs for these men.

He wrote:

> No machinery exists in the normal process of a liquidation on this scale for caring for these men to their own and the community's advantage. So what is to be done? It may seem naive to suggest that they might best be applied to the task they are trained for - building ships - for a limited, but substantially longer, period than the nine months or so required to work out contracts at Clydebank and Scotstoun.

His 'quite special sort of company' would contain the parts of U.C.S. not required by the Govan/Linthouse company. It would not in all likelihood be profitable, said Macmichael, but it need not be heavily loss-making. Orders would not be difficult to get since there would be a Government-backed guarantee of delivery.

Davies had poured cold water on the idea when it was put to him, arguing that there would be problems of competition between the two. But Macmichael argued that rather than the two companies being totally separate there would be a business relationship between them. They would share certain services, such as administration, but to keep strict control of costs the two would have to be accounted separately.

Macmichael - by no means a socialist - ended his Herald article:

> Some such formula is going to be increasingly necessary if the Government sticks to its 'lame duck' philosophy. Refusal to support lame ducks sounds all right when they are limited liability companies.
> There are no lamer ducks, however, than men on the dole, and these we do support. The logic seems to break down somewhere along the line.

It is worth mentioning that the stewards made some attempt to go some way towards this proposal. James Reid suggested the change and put it to Sir John Eden, the Minister for Industry, at a meeting on 9 August. It was to put the whole consortium on a five-year experimental period, in which time it could either prove itself or go to the wall. They could not accept a phased run-down but they were willing to go one better than Wilson and prove the yards' viability in five years.

This did not become the fixed policy of the stewards but was put forward as a basis for negotiation. Sir John Eden declined to put the proposal to the Cabinet.

Nor was he attracted to the Clydeside Development Authority proposed by the Trades Union Congress. The C.D.A. plan had been agreed with the stewards and the S.T.U.C. by Vic Feather, the T.U.C. General Secretary, while he was in Glasgow to address both a special congress of the S.T.U.C. and a mass demonstration by the stewards. The full interest shown by the T.U.C. in the future of one company was possibly the most exciting aspect of the summer of 1971.

The congress had always fought the question of redundancy or closure on a national scale, leaving specific cases either to the unions involved or local officials and stewards. Never before had the T.U.C. committed itself so fully to a fight against one closure. That it gave such support to a Communist-led stewards' movement made its involvement remarkable.

Only months before the T.U.C. General Council had refused to take part in a one-day strike against legislation striking at the roots of trade unionism. Now Vic Feather had come to Glasgow to march arm-in-arm with thousands of workers who had downed tools to protest against the redundancies of one company.

Vic Feather's involvement added much to the campaign. He added the weight of the 10,000,000 workers affiliated to the T.U.C. behind the stewards, and by so doing removed any last traces of stigma or doubt about the personalities involved, and their motives. But more than that, he widened the intent and the strength of the campaign.

The stewards had been zealous in holding on to the leadership of the fight. It wasn't just a question of not trusting the established leaders of the trade unions, there was also an argument in the west of Scotland that the campaign should be widened to include a fight against all redundancies. The U.C.S. men, afraid of a dissipation of effort, argued that the first priority must be to win their case. After that the other fights would be easier because the Government's 'lame duck' policy would have been smashed.

Vic Feather managed to produce a formula which both the stewards and those from many other hard hit factories in the Clyde industrial belt could put their full energies into.

He first outlined his proposal at a recall congress of the S.T.U.C. on the subject of unemployment in the Partick Burgh Hall, Glasgow, on 16 August. It was a historic occasion. Never before had the S.T.U.C. been recalled. General Secretary James Jack told the delegates: 'Not even during the long and hungry thirties, when unemployment was about 18 per cent and sometimes as high as 28 per cent, was one called. '

Protocol was also broken to allow Jimmy Reid to speak. He got a standing ovation when he said: 'It is about time the working class and the trade union movement had a charter of rights, at the heart of which is the "Right to Work". If the Government or the social system cannot give us that right then we must change the Government or modify the system. '

Feather's plan for a Clydeside Development Authority was an extension to the Special Development Area status already affecting the west of Scotland The C.D.A. was a more far-reaching and positive concept. Feather said: 'One of the first jobs of the Authority would be to take over all the assets and liabilities of U.C.S. and seek sufficient new orders to keep employment at approximately the present level for the immediate future. '

But, he said, if the Authority, on examination, concluded that some men could be better used outside U.C.S. then it would ensure that nobody would become redundant unless there was sufficient investment to provide alternative, 'and at least equally productive', employment. In a nutshell the C.D.A. would take over Macmichael's suggested task of a massive programme of retraining and redeployment, and in the meantime would have the money and the power to keep men employed gainfully.

The C.D.A. was not intended to be a trade union body, but should include employers and local authority representatives. It would be financed by an initial grant plus interest free loans from the Exchequer. Feather refused to be drawn on the cost of such an ambitious scheme but it could be well over the £25 million mark.

Feather was successful in getting the men to agree with the concept. Till then they had been very strict in saying that not a man should 'go down the road'. Now Reid was talking in terms of 'no redundancies unless there is alternative work'.

These plans involved a Government control and social involvement in the yards. There were others who felt the advisory committee had been wrong and that they could make a commercial go of the doomed yards.

The first sign of commercial interest in Clydebank came from Scottish millionaire Archibald 'cashdown' Kelly. Mr. Kelly is a fifty-year-old ship repairer with a reputation for making profits out of enterprises he bought while they were in financial straits. He gained the name 'cashdown' from his liking for keeping large sums of money in the bank in order to pay bills in cash.

He had bought the Ardrossan Dockyard in Ayrshire when it got into difficulties and sold it a few years later for a profit. He had used the yard at first for his ship-repairing business, but sold it to the Clyde Port Authority who are converting most of it into a terminal for car ferries. The rest is filled in for building development.

He then bought the Liffey dockyard in Dublin, once again a yard in trouble, for about £250, 000 in cash. It is now profitable though strictly small time, employing just over 100 men. Similar bids to buy larger companies, such as the Manchester Dry Docks Company were unsuccessful.

Within days of liquidation, Kelly expressed an interest to the provisional liquidator in taking over the Clydebank division. His plan was to knock down the older east yard leaving the two slipways on the west for building ships. A new dry dock would be built on the east site for fitting and repairing. Although the buying market was in decline there was a shortage of dock and fitting out facilities in the world.

He had £1 million in his bank account to put into the project, but made no bones about the fact that it could not get off the ground without Government help. Because he was so early into the field the stewards refused to discuss his plans with him. Their original policy - later altered by events - was to keep the yards together. 'We will talk to anyone who wishes to keep all the yards together with the present labour force, ' said James Airlie.

Then events took a strange turn. During a meeting

between Kelly and Sir John Eden, the Scot got the impression that he was being asked to take over all the yards by the Government. He flew back to Glasgow full of hope and said he would try to raise the money from private sources. Now the stewards agreed to talk and for several days a feeling of excitement rose as Airlie, Reid and Sam Barr flew up to Kelly's holiday mansion on the Hebridean island of Islay. 'A Summit meeting' said the Scottish Daily Express who had chartered the plane to take the stewards to Kelly!

Although Kelly did not give a guarantee of employment to the current labour force the talks were very amicable. For the next few days there were meetings in accountants' offices in Glasgow; crowds gathered in the street outside. The scene had all the atmosphere of an eleventh-hour rescue.

But it all crashed down when Kelly went back to see Eden. The Minister stuck by his Govan / Linthouse scheme and, it appears, had only been asking if Kelly would be willing to put money into that.*

Everyone reacted bitterly. Kelly blamed both the unions and the Government for the knock-back. 'To guarantee no redundancies and no contractions is very difficult,' he said. Later he added, 'If the Government is set on closing down U.C.S. they are going the right way about it.' He withdrew his bid for Clydebank, though after the Govan Shipbuilders company began to talk hopefully about Scotstoun, he put it back in.

By then, however, a larger and better financed body had taken an interest in the Clydebank yard. Breaksea Tankships Inc. of Houston, Texas expressed an interest

---

*Sir John Eden seems to be unlucky in making his meaning clear. A few weeks later he was reported to have said in Sheffield that people were becoming too obsessed with unemployment. He denied that he had meant that either!

in buying the yard in order to convert it to the building of special ships designed for carrying liquid natural gas. The company, with extensive financial connections in Europe and North America planned to build four £25 million gas tankers a year in the yard and would certainly need at least the present work force. Clydebank under U.C.S. became one of the premier yards in the world for the production of oil rigs, so the men have already proved themselves adaptable to new techniques and designs.

In all the emotional upset surrounding fears for the future of Clydebank, the fate of Scotstoun yard, with 1,200 men, tended to become obscured. The yard had belonged to the <u>Connell family</u> before the creation of U.C.S. and Charles Connell was still a divisional director for Scotstoun. He and his father, Sir Charles, called a press conference on the eve of the announcement of the board of Govan Shipbuilders, to announce their renewed interest in the yard.

The basis of their optimism lay in their claim that theirs was the only yard, by virtue of the geography of the river at Scotstoun, able to build the Panamax. The Panamax is a U.C.S. design for a 77,000-ton bulk carrier and is the largest size of ship able to negotiate the Panama canal. Extensive rebuilding would have to take place at Govan to accommodate a ship of that size.

Indeed, said the Connells, their number two berth could be extended to launch 117,000 or even 145,000-ton ships, much larger than the Govan potential. Such a scheme, if feasible, would mean more employment not less. Mr. Connell said: 'With 1,080 feet of water to launch into, Scotstoun has the best and most flexible berth on the Upper Clyde.'

To back up their claims they produced detailed production figures for the yard. According to their figures the yard had produced, on an equivalent basis, 23 per cent more steel per 1,000 workers than any other U.C.S. division. It had, they said, only lost 3.37 per cent of the total U.C.S. loss. It was the first yard in Britain to introduce 'Relaxation of

Working Practices', the agreement with the boiler-makers which began the end of demarcation problems in shipbuilding.

Ken Douglas too went on record as saying that he could make the yard profitable if someone was to give it to him with some working capital. He regarded the facilities at Scotstoun as no better or worse than those he had found at Austin and Pickersgill where he had run the company very successfully. Unlike the Connells he did not stipulate that the Scotstoun yard would have to be included with Govan/Linthouse before it could be viable.

However the Government showed no interest in the Connell plan. Sir Charles described their reaction as 'about as impenetrable as a stone wall'.

Finally, in the course of events, evidence appeared that no lesser personages than the <u>liquidator</u> AND the <u>Government</u> disagreed with the pessimism of the 'Four Wise Men'!

In response to the interest shown in Clydebank by Archie Kelly, Mr. Smith, the liquidator, issued a statement on 19 August. Much of it has relevance to the other proposals for the future of the consortium. It said:

> I have also recognised that the interest of any potential purchasers would depend on three factors:
>
> 1. The availability of financial support through existing Government agencies.
>
> 2. An unbroken flow of work in progress with the prospect of future orders at profitable prices.
>
> 3. The existence of a workforce appropriate to the shipbuilding needs of the yards...
>
> I have tried to secure the second condition by the logical progression of work on hand, and by keeping open contracts on which I have neither the authority

or resources to embark. Equally important, and perhaps more difficult, has been the task of maintaining in owners, present and future, some degree of confidence in the Clyde.

Not much sign there of a willingness to axe the unwanted yards or to concentrate the order book at Govan/Linthouse. In fact he emphasised: 'Given the confidence of the owners - and that is an inescapable essential - I see no need to talk of the closure of any of the yards. I never have.'

No Government Minister was actually caught admitting a lack of confidence in the findings of the 'Four Wise Men'. But it is not without significance that only four months after the advisory committee had conducted a feasibility study of the yards and the Cabinet had accepted their conclusions, further Government sponsored feasibility studies of Clydebank and Scotstoun were started.

It took a month for each 'Wise Man's' credibility to be destroyed.

X

'THEY WILL BE IN AT WORK ON MONDAY'

Thursday 5 August 1971 was a poor day for democracy
in Britain. The OZ trial sentences were announced;
the Education (Milk) Act became law; the first full
session of Ted Heath's Government ended. And the
Industrial Relations Act received the Royal Assent.

The first positive act to break that law was the
mass U.C.S. demonstration in Glasgow thirteen days
later, on Wednesday the 18th. Although it was law,
none of the agencies created by it had yet been
set up. So there was no way of imposing any penalties
for breaking the Act.

Not that the Clydeside marchers were worried. If
the Act was going to be challenged then nobody there
that day doubted that this was the time and the issue
on which to fight it.

Scotland has not seen a march like it in living
memory. Not since the days of the Chartists in 1848
did so many people take to the streets of Glasgow.
When the front stewards arrived at Glasgow Green
there were marchers still leaving George Square,
two miles away. Estimates of those taking part
varied from 60,000 to 80,000.

Four train loads came from Clydebank, one
carrying mainly women and children. Every major
factory in the west of Scotland stopped work, involving
over 160,000 workers. The sea of banners
represented every section of the Labour movement.
There were many Scottish Nationalist Party flags and
placards. There were banners from the south,
Birmingham, Wolverhampton and London. The Fleet
Street electricians brought their embroidered banner

and a £400 cheque. Labour M.P.s, used to marching behind many banners in their time brought their own for the first time. It read 'Scottish Labour M.P.s support U.C.S.'.

The placards reflected the good humour of the crowds lining every part of the route. Only twenty-four hours after the international horse rider Harvey Smith had been disqualified for giving a judge the two-fingered salute, a banner read 'A Harvey Smith to Heath'. Another read 'Give Heath an inch and he takes a yard'.

At the meeting of west of Scotland stewards the week before, in the Partick Bingo Hall, the only dissenting voice from the plan for a march was Clydebank minister the Rev. Alex Lawson. He argued the loss of production a stoppage would create would alienate fringe supporters like himself.

But if the reverend wasn't happy, somebody up there must have been smiling on the workers for a two-week spell of rain was punctuated by a day of brilliant sunshine for the demo. As the marchers set off from George Square, opposition came from Glasgow's Lord Provost, Sir Donald Liddle.

Sir Donald, a progressive councillor and a city clothing manufacturer, had been elected Provost during a short period of power by the right-wing alliance in Glasgow Corporation. He had been genuinely worried about the effects of closure and had joined many lobbies at Westminster by leading citizens from Glasgow. He also attended the very militant variety show put on by Equity to raise funds for the Fighting Fund. Indeed at a dinner with Ted Heath, he went out of his way to tell the P.M. that the people of Clydeside were getting impatient and saw a black cloud - 'and it's not a morning one ' - hanging over the area.

Yet he refused to sign the men's petition, saying that people knew where he stood on the subject. And, at the airport hotel opening, he chose to go in by another door, avoiding the U.C.S. picket. On the day of the march, the evening papers in Glasgow splashed his remarks that the loss of production was 'not

clever and that he would have preferred a weekend
march, in the interests of the men who had given up
a day's wages.

It seemed that the rest of Glasgow disagreed with
their civic leader and turned up. At Glasgow Green
there were so many people round the platform and
so many film crews and photographers inside the
fenced off press enclosure that the scene was
reminiscent of a pop festival.

Fencing had been put round the platform because
of heckling at the previous march in June. 'Ultra',
according to Reid, or 'bamsticks' according to Airlie,
anyway left-wing militants, had stationed themselves
in front of the platform long before the marchers had
arrived and had then tried to shout down Benn.

This time pride of place was given to the U.C.S.
stewards. On the platform were the conveners and
the long list of speakers. The crowd stood in the hot
sun in the middle of the Glasgow park on the spot
where so many famour Labour leaders and 'Red
Clydesiders' had spoken; where ex-servicemen fought
and won a pitched battle with police during the 'Forty-
Hour' strike of 1919; where Mosley was thrown off the
platform in 1932, never to return to speak in Glasgow
again.

Of the speakers that day only one revived the
atmosphere and the emotions of those days of oratory
and revolution. At the microphone were Benn, Feather,
McGarvey, Scanlon of the A.E.U., William Ross,
Billy Wolfe of the S.N.P., James Jack of the S.T.U.C.
and Alex Murray of the Scottish Communist Party. But
despite the bevy of political talent, the man the crowd
had come to hear and cheer was Jimmy Reid.

He spoke in his shirt sleeves, without notes, and
holding onto the microphone like a pub singer. His
speech was easily the most militant and the most
welcome to the crowd. He told them that the first 160
men to be sacked had received their notices, but
added slowly: 'They will be in at work on Monday.'
A sea of clenched fists punched the air as an exultant
roar went up.

The only incident came when a long haired man in

105

his late thirties threw a roll of lighted film onto the platform while Benn was speaking. Stewards had to leap into the crowd to rescue him from angry marchers.

It did not succeed in even denting the strong and beautiful solidarity of the day. Few people thought a about it at the time, but the first blow against the Industrial Relations Act had been well and truly struck.

For a few days after, it looked as though events were beginning to speed up. Vic Feather met Sir John Eden in London (Davies was on holiday in the South of France) and put the C.D.A. plan to him. After the meeting it was announced that Eden was flying to Glasgow and would be meeting stewards and S.T.U.C. Officials. The talks went on till 1 a.m. in the Central Hotel, but there was still no movement on either side. Eden flew on to the island of Mull, off the west coast of Scotland for a few days rest.

The spirit of the Upper Clyde workers began to spread. Workers at the Plessey factory, in Alexandria, Dunbartonshire, decided to take action after being paid off and the factory closed. The town is only a few miles from Clydebank and had a male unemployment figure of 10 per cent. Over 400 children left schools in that part of Dunbartonshire without jobs to go to that summer. The only major employer for the town, apart from Plessey, was U.C.S.

Unlike the U.C.S. men, the Plessey workers could not 'work-in'. The type of work they did prevented this. In a shipyard there is still work to complete months after the day of liquidation. In an electronics and light engineering factory like Plessey's there is no demand for goods produced even minutes after liquidation. In any case, the middle and senior management left on the last day and there was no organisation in the factory.

The men decided to occupy the factory to prevent the capital equipment being removed to the Plessey main works at Ilford. They argued that the equipment had mostly been paid for by the Government as an incentive to Plessey, only twelve months previously, who opened a branch factory in the town in the former Government Torpedo factory. The equipment, they

106

said, would be looked after by them for the next employer willing to open up in Alexandria. When the managers drove out on the Friday, the men locked the gates, pulled down the company flag and began a round-the-clock occupation. The U.C.S. men sent them £250 to sustain their struggle.

On the day of occupation, the shipowners with orders at U.C.S. went to see Nicholas Ridley at the D.O.T.I. Of the twenty-nine orders on the U.C.S. books at liquidation, work had been started on fifteen - six fitting out, eight on the slipways and ship 121 in the pre-fabrication stage. After liquidation the owners had agreed with Mr. Smith that they would await the outcome of political developments before considering taking their orders elsewhere, but time was now pressing.

So, on Friday 28 August they told Ridley that unless there was some sign of Government action soon, they would be forced to place their contracts elsewhere. They wanted guarantees of completion, delivery dates and maintenance of the original price agreed with U.C.S.

Ridley replied that he could not give any guarantees before the Govan/Linthouse company had been got off the ground. That would not happen, he said, till the unions agreed to the Government conditions of 'competitive wage rates' and changes in working practices.

The owners told him bluntly that they had now been forced to make preliminary enquiries round the market to see if there were other possibilities for their orders. They had in fact been approached by some foreign yards looking for the work. But the Under Secretary could not budge. As he left the meeting, Mr. Perry Greer of the Irish Shipping Company, whose four orders were most immediate, told reporters: 'Mr. Ridley did not seem too alarmed at what we had to tell him'.

Five weeks later, when the company sent a letter to Davies re-iterating their position, the Minister reacted in horror and issued an ultimatum to the unions saying he was under tremendous pressure to release the contracts. The company retorted that their letter had not been intended to be a final demand.

By now the liquidator was beginning to lay off men. He did not, however, follow the plan he had announced at the press conference on the day the yards were taken over. Instead of the 400 who were to be laid off immediately there were various weekly redundancies in dribs and drabs - 220 this week, sixty-four the next. The workers imposed an overtime ban as soon as the first cards went out which helped alleviate some of the need for redundancies. But there could be no question of the workforce going slow in order to create jobs. The bonus rate for steelworkers actually went up by 4p an hour the week after the takeover.

The volume of work and support put heavy pressure on the stewards. Treasurer Roddy McKenzie was getting so much mail that three Clydebank yard officeworkers were seconded to the committee to help. They were all eventually laid off themselves - including Mrs. Isobel Dickie, the wife of the yard convener - and joined the 'work-in' to work out pay rates and insurance stamps for their colleagues 'working in'.

The technical problems involved meant that sub-committees had to be created. There was an organisation sub-committee for work problems, a campaign committee to deal with the hundreds of requests for speakers, a publicity sub-committee to organise the vast volume of literature put out inside and outside the yards, and a finance sub-committee.

The whole resources of Clydebank town council were now being utilised by the campaign. The council dustcarts drove round the town with U.C.S. posters stuck on them. The manager of the municipal bank became the Fighting Fund accountant. The police committee maintained the policeman at the yard gates to direct traffic after the liquidator ceased to pay his wages.

But as time went on the pressure to get together across a table was growing. Public opinion was forcing John Davies; and the official trade union movement, especially Dan McGarvey, was forcing the stewards.

Despite his Clydeside background there was little love lost between the Scottish shop-floor boilermakers' stewards and their president. There is still resentment over the union's role in the closure of the shipyard at Grangemouth on Scotland's east coast. As a signatory to the Cameron Inquiry into the bitter union struggle in the famous Barbican building dispute, he earned the strong dislike of the Left.

From the beginning of the crisis, it had been emphasised again and again in private discussion that when negotiations escalated to the involvement of the official trade union leadership, the stewards would have to be very vigilant of negotiated compromises.

It is in the nature of things for officials to compromise and shop floor representatives to cry 'sell out' - it is, in a sense, what they are both elected to do. But, in the U.C.S. struggle, there was no more wary and nervous coalition between stewards and officials of the fourteen unions involved than that between the boilermakers and their leader.

So with all that nervousness about, it is surprising that the stewards should have decided not to send representatives to a meeting between Davies and both McGarvey and Jack Service in their capacities as President and General Secretary of the 'Confed.' on Tuesday 31 August.

McGarvey had told the stewards by telephone that the meeting was to discuss 'procedure' for future meetings - talks about talks. The decision not to send was backed by Reid and Airlie who argued that if anything else was discussed which involved the yards, there could be no decisions without the support of the stewards and ultimately the work force.

Why they should have thought that the Secretary of State for Trade and Industry and the President and General Secretary of the 'Confed.' would only discuss 'procedure' when they got together round a table is a mystery. Perhaps the continued tactical victories of the previous ten weeks bred a false sense of confidence or perhaps they did not want to be a party to any 'sell out' that might be reached. Either way it was a mistake.

A startled Reid was phoned at home that evening by the Glasgow Herald to tell him that McGarvey had said, on leaving the meeting at the D.O.T.I. that the unions would be willing to concede three-shift working if the four yards could be kept going. The next day McGarvey assured the stewards that he had been misquoted and had not offered three-shift working to Davies.

Nevertheless, a full stewards' meeting decided to send Reid and Airlie to another meeting between Davies and McGarvey in London on the following Monday. It was stressed by several speakers, and agreed by the two representatives, that there would be no question of them sitting in another room in order to be available for consultation, as is normal in union Government negotiations. 'If we are not in at that table, we leave,' said Airlie.

In the event, though, the two stewards never reached that negotiating table. McGarvey told them it was his job to talk to Davies, who had insisted on this procedure. The two men had a quick discussion and decided to accept the position for the time being. They felt, correctly, that if they walked out, the press would seize on a split between the union side.

At future talks they were in attendance, but by then McGarvey had asserted his leadership of the negotiations and it was very much his show from then on.

But there were still a few acts to go before the finale.

Enter a smiling Prime Minister - stage right.

XI

'ENTER A SMILING PRIME MINISTER
- STAGE RIGHT'

If John Davies is the Buster Keaton of the U.C.S.
saga - 'The Face that Sank a Hundred Ships' - then
Edward Heath is the Tommy Cooper.

His visit to Glasgow in September 1971 turned to
comic disaster as trick after trick failed. The five-
hour trip did nothing to better either the U.C.S
situation or the Prime Minister's image.

He squeezed in a trip to Glasgow on 10 September
between visits to the opera and ballet at the Edinburgh
Festival. When he arrived at the opera he was cheered
by worthy Edinburgh citizens, in gratitude for the
£$2\frac{1}{4}$ million grant from the Government towards the
cost of a new opera house for the city.

In Glasgow, crowds turned out to greet Mr. Heath,
but this time there were no cheers. About 250 U.C.S.
and Plessey workers gathered outside the Central
Hotel, where Ted was to speak, with their banners
and a very gentlemanly cheer leader. A Plessey
steward had brought a hand loudhailer and led the
waiting men in chants of, 'If you hate Edward Heath
clap your hands', and songs like 'Teddy's taking us
to the Buroo tomorrow', based on the current pop
song. As each chant or song ended, the steward
politely said 'Thank You' and clicked off.

The visit had been planned months before to
allow Heath a chance to address the party's faithful
on the Common Market before the Conservative
annual conference in Brighton. The pressure on the
Government over U.C.S. had built up so tremendously
in the meantime that it was impossible to avoid
speaking on the subject in Glasgow.

111

John Davies in Glasgow on 6 August

Edward Heath

Expectations, encouraged by Government press officers, were running high that Heath would announce a new move in the situation. For two weeks before his visit, industrial correspondents in the west of Scotland had been writing that the new Govan/Linthouse board would be announced 'in a few days'. Davies had twice been up on secret visits to Scotland and was obviously having difficulty finding anyone willing to head the new company. Then it was announced that Heath would make a major speech on Scottish industry at a special luncheon in Glasgow. It seemed that an announcement on U.C.S. would be made.

The lunch was held in the huge Central Hotel and over 150 leading west of Scotland citizens were invited. There were industrialists, trade unionists, M.P.s, councillors. It had all the signs of a new initiative. One minute no Government Ministers could be seen for love or money; now the Prime Minister was gathering together for a lunch all those people who had been screaming - or in some cases, whispering - blue murder since the U.C.S. crisis began.

Unfortunately the build-up fizzled out in a big let down. Heath had nothing fresh to say. His speech was dull and there were no new announcements. Instead there was a litany of the root evils at work in Scotland, dependence on declining heavy industry, no 'headquarter based industries', a steady rise over five years in unemployment. The answer, apparently, was to be arrived at between local authorities, employers and the trade unions. The Government was doing its bit by taking us into the Common Market and increasing the money for house and school building and an expanded road programme.

He repeated part of a speech he made in Dundee in 1969: 'We refuse to condemn large parts of the kingdom to slow decline and decay, to dereliction and persistent unemployment in pursuit of old-fangled nineteenth-century doctrines of laisser-faire.'

However, on U.C.S. it seemed that there was little he could do but stick by the advisory committee report and laisse Clydebank and Scotstoun faire as best they could. No Scottish paper bothered to quote the speech the next day, apart from the <u>Express</u> who remarked on Mr. Heath's reading of the speech. They noted that he even read out 'Lockhead' for 'Lockheed' when a misprint appeared in the text.

There were several empty seats at the lunch. Most Labour magistrates in Glasgow boycotted the event and only five Labour M.P.s turned up. Alex Kitson of the S.T.U.C. had left the T.U.C. in Blackpool early to attend the lunch. He sat two seats away from Heath.

Before the lunch he approached Scottish Under-Secretary, George Younger, requesting a meeting between Heath and two stewards. He naturally expected that, as the representative of the trade union movement in Scotland, he would be present at the meeting.

But when the two stewards - David Reid and Sam Gilmore, who had not been at the dinner - went up to suite 290, together with Kitson and Clydebank M.P. Hugh McCartney, to meet the P.M., they were told Heath would see them alone. Kitson had argued that Heath should see the two men because they had actually been declared redundant and were 'working-in'. Now the P.M.'s aides said Heath would only speak to the two men about their redundancies; the meeting was not about the wider issues of unemployment.

A fierce argument then developed between Kitson, who had already been angered by the speech, and the aides, with occasional interventions from the many detectives present.

As Kitson stormed up and down arguing with everyone he could find with some responsibility for keeping him out, the whole press contingent and T.V. cameras were watching the amazing scene.

One minute Kitson would be angrily shouting at Heath's press officer, the next he would stride down the passage to tell us what was happening. As he got more and more frustrated the argument got louder and louder. Kitson took it as a slight on the S.T.U.C. that he was not being included. The Prime Minister was inside the suite talking to party treasurer Hugh

Stenhouse and must have been able to hear the battle.

Kitson shouted at an aide who had emerged to once again tell him he was not welcome: 'I am here as the official representative of the S.T.U.C., yet the Prime Minister will not see me? No Prime Minister has ever come to Scotland before and refused to see the S.T.U.C.' He suggested as a compromise that he go in as an observer with the stewards, without joining in the discussion, but this too was rejected.

By this time he was practically jumping up and down in rage. He came down the hall to tell us that apparently Heath had been happy to 'let us eat his fucking chips but he won't talk to us about unemployment.'

The seize was then complicated with the arrival of another four Labour M.P.s - Dickson Mabon, a former Minister of State for Scotland, Greenock; Ian Campbell, West Dunbartonshire; James White, Pollok; and John Rankin, Govan. They had arrived also to seek a meeting with Heath to discuss the T.U.C.'s plan for a C.D.A.

The whole comedy started again. Mabon got into a heated argument with the P.M.'s press officer Mr. Henry James. It was quite a busy last day in the position for James who was leaving to become the press officer at the Ministry for the Environment. Both he and two nervously grinning Scottish Office officials had to take all the shouting and anger from the M.P.s and Kitson without being able to reply in kind. A solid phalanx of newsmen stood at the end of the corridor eagerly waiting for any insult or heated reply from any of Heath's staff.

An incident nearly arose when Mabon, a neat wee Scots doctor, said to an obstinate James: 'The Prime Minister won't see his colleagues from parliament? This is ridiculous. Who are you to tell me that I can't see him?' James replied quietly, 'There is no need to be offensive.' 'Don't call me offensive,' shouted Mabon. 'I am not being offensive. If the Prime Minister will not discuss U.C.S. let him come out here and tell us himself - not send someone else.'

Eventually the two stewards, who had stayed in the background during the arguments, went in to see

Heath alone for thirty minutes. Outside, the angry, but unsuccessful, suitors went off to hold a press conference elsewhere in the building.

The meeting between Heath and the two men ran a predictable course that had, once again, its comic side. Gilmore prodded the Prime Minister on the amount of time he spent sailing. 'But,' protested Heath, 'sailing gives me energy to take decisions.' Later when Gilmore suggested he spend more time in Whitehall and less chasing dolphins, Heath became annoyed and insisted he had been working 'like a black' since he came to power. 'We'll have none of that Powellism here,' Gilmore told him.

By then the Heath road show was running an hour behind its time. When he had arrived at the hotel he had had to pass through the ranks of demonstrators. He left his car and was swept towards the hotel's revolving doors by a phalanx of detectives. As the car approached, the shouting rose to a roar.

Then, for the first time, I had an insight into the feelings an unpopular politician must experience when he has to walk through a crowd of people who hate him completely.

I was standing next to the hotel entrance as the Prime Minister walked past, and the crowd seemed to sway as one in his direction. All the time he was smiling broadly and as he reached the door he turned to look at the crowd. For one frightening moment, I thought he was going to wave to them.

Fortunately he did not. The U.C.S. men were all redundant and were now 'working-in' and, of course, the Plessey men were unemployed. They might have misinterpreted a cheery wave.

Now, as he was leaving, most of the crowds, and with them the tension, had gone. A few people were still standing about waiting for a chance to see Heath. He still maintained a brisk walking pace and headed towards his car flashing as big a smile as ever.

He did, however, miss one 'fan' who had run out from the crowd. A middle-aged man ran towards him shouting, 'Heath Out'. A large Glasgow 'polisman' caught him in full flights and threw him back into the crowd.

The man was released after the Prime Minister left. Trying to belt the Premier was apparently not a crime in Glasgow during the U.C.S. crisis!

The following weekend a secret meeting between Davies and top Scottish businessmen took place in a Troon hotel, overlooking the picturesque Clyde coast. Davies flew up with Eden and senior D.O.T.I. officials. Campbell flew down from Inverness. The Scots included Lord Clydesmuir, chairman of the Scottish Council (Development and Industry); Matthew Wylie, chairman of the C.B.I. in Scotland; Robert Smith, the U.C.S. liquidator. Hugh Stenhouse, the insurance tycoon and Archibald Gilchrist of Brown Brothers, an Edinburgh engineering firm, were also there.

The group were told that Stenhouse and Gilchrist had managed to raise £1 million as starting capital for a new firm based on Govan/Linthouse. It was to be called Govan Shipbuilders Ltd. with Stenhouse as chairman and Gilchrist as managing director.

It appeared that the long chat Heath had had with Stenhouse in the Central Hotel on the 10th had been about more than the latter's functions as treasurer of the Conservative Party in Scotland.

The announcement was scheduled for a D.O.T.I. press conference in London that Wednesday. But on the Tuesday morning the Glasgow Herald leaked the pending appointments. The news caused a furore over both the choice of Stenhouse and the fact that Douglas, long tipped for a senior job in the new company and certainly the most able for it, had been overlooked.

Douglas had been playing a very quiet game during the crisis. Unlike Hepper, who left immediately, he had stayed on to assist the liquidator tidy up the affairs of the company.

He did not come out in public support or sympathy with the 'work-in' but he was known to be in close touch with the stewards behind the scenes. There is no doubt that the claim made by Reid - and hotly denied by the D.O.T.I. - that there had been £100 million worth of orders in the pipeline, came from Douglas. He met with the leading stewards at regular intervals.

There can be no doubt, on the other hand, that Douglas was a career shipbuilder and was not going to jeopardise his future for the 'work-in'. He was asked by the stewards at one private meeting to become 'managing director' of Upper Clyde Shipyard Workers Unlimited, but declined.

By mid-September it was clear that the Government's dislike of U.C.S. and its determination to end it included Ken Douglas. Just as the stewards' campaign was keeping Ridley in a job (to sack him would have been seen as capitulation), so did the praise from the stewards keep Douglas from a job.

At long last in September, Douglas came out in open support of the 'work-in' by giving his first interview since the crisis to a broadsheet produced for the stewards. The Co-operative press printed 100,000 copies free and the Glasgow Branch of the National Union of Journalists provided the copy.

In the interview the former managing director was scathing in his rebuttal of the Ridley Report. He pointed out that it had been based on a one-hour meeting with himself and Hepper and it was a 'biased and prejudiced report'. Of Ridley's comment that he was not impressed by the management, he said, 'The feeling is mutual'.

Stenhouse as chairman was also unpopular. Not only was he a high ranking Tory party official - leading to the assumption that he had taken on the job more out of duty than economic desire - but he was not regarded as being either expert or interested in shipbuilding. He had been a member of the board during the Fairfields Experiment but that too had probably been more a matter of duty than profit. The Glasgow Herald commented: 'Mr. Stenhouse, we suspect, has taken on this new responsibility because others would not accept it.'

Hugh Cowan Stenhouse at 56 was one of the richest men in Scotland. Unlike most Scots who are involved in big business he refused to move to London. He

Edward Heath leaving the Central Hotel in Glasgow

Hugh Stenhouse in his Glasgow office

built up a company inherited from his father into a
company worth over £50 million with interests
including textiles and property as well as the main
insurance business. There are few stronger supporters
of a minimum interference by government in the
affairs of industry and commerce.

He was an aggressive Scot with a bullying attitude to
reporters who questioned his motives. Suggestions of
surprise that he had put aside his profit motive for
Clydeside patriotism in taking on U.C.S. were met
with an outraged 'How dare you think that?' look.
There can have been few shrewder businessmen.

He had a great interest in the plan to develop an
industrial centre on the Clyde coast at Hunterston
where the deep water facilities are second to none.
A few weeks before being talked into taking on U.C.S.
he started another company, again backed by the
Government to study the potential of Hunterston. At
present there is a nuclear power station and there
are plans for a £1,000 million steel complex linked
with an ore and oil terminal. Obviously a large market
for such a steel complex would be shipbuilding.

This interest led to criticism when it became known
Stenhouse was taking over Govan/Linthouse. For only
two months before, while receiving an honorary
degree from Strathclyde University he had said: 'We
should have stopped launching ships into the narrow
waters of the river years ago. Our shipyards ought
to have been building oceanships on the ocean shore,
leading shipping rather than being led by it'. In a
reference to U.C.S. he added that the men's jobs
would not be in jeopardy if the yards had been based
at Hunterston.

Now criticism was levelled at his appointment by
many who felt that not only had the job been taken
by him and offered to him because of his position in
the Scottish Conservative Party; but that he had no
real faith in the future of shipbuilding on the upper
reaches.

After the Herald leak on the Tuesday, Stenhouse
insisted that the press conference to announce the
appointments should be held in Glasgow. This time

Davies brought Eden, Campbell, and several top civil servants with him. They sat around him at the top of the long conference table in the elegant Satinwood Salon in the City Chambers.

The Minister was put under pressure by the industrial correspondents on the future of Douglas. He claimed that before Douglas had gone on holiday, he had given the Minister an assurance that he would give every assistance to the new company.

But the press were insistent. Was Douglas to be offered a job? Davies insisted that it was up to Stenhouse to make any appointments and Stenhouse said he could not say anything till he saw Douglas after he returned from holiday. 'Surely,' said Jack McGill of the Express, 'it is possible to telephone 800 miles to Majorca?' But there was no response to that.

Stenhouse and Gilchrist announced that they intended to go to the Linthouse division that afternoon to talk to the liquidator. The stewards had said they would not admit them, so at 2 p.m. a large contingent of newsmen and stewards gathered at the gates.

Stenhouse borrowed his secretary's green Morris 1300 to drive himself and his colleague to the yard. He felt that it was not the correct image to arrive in his chauffeur-driven Daimler. His compromise for appearance's sake did not extend to taking his secretary's Conservative Party sticker off the windscreen.

The two men parked ten yards from the closed main gates and got out. The crowd parted as they walked up to Airlie who was standing with his arms folded on the other side of the wire mesh. The gate was opened a few feet to allow him to step out to meet them.

Stenhouse asked first, 'Can we come in?' Airlie told him that the stewards accepted that they had come as private individuals to see the liquidator and as such they would be allowed in. But he added: 'I would ask you to make alternative arrangements in future to see the liquidator elsewhere outside the yards.

'Our position is that we are in charge of the yards and we decide who gets through the gates. We are not co-operating with any Government boards.'

Hugh Stenhouse was killed tragically in a car crash on 25 November 1971. However, since then, the Government has given an assurance that Govan Shipbuilders Ltd. will continue and they are presently looking for a new chairman.

XII

THE END OF THE BEGINNING

From the beginning the stewards had been wary of any
moves that might, even slightly, come within the
description of sensationalism. Their publicity machine
was second to none and could not have been bettered
by any professional agency.

But the policy was to be responsibility, and the
wilder excesses of newsmen, especially photographers,
were frequently turned down. I remember putting up
the idea at the beginning of the 'work-in' that a banner
reading 'Under New Management' be placed above the
U.C.S. sign across the entrance to Govan yard.

My point was that it would lift the morale of
the Govan men who were returning that week from
holiday, as well as making a tremendous picture for
every front page in the country. At first Airlie liked
the idea but it was squashed by Reid who stood up and
said simply with a dismissive sweep of his hand,
'Gimmickry!'. The idea was dropped.

For the same reasons the stewards had resisted
the temptation to hold their committee meetings in
the company boardroom. The spoken reason was
that it was not a good issue on which to have a fight
with the liquidator. Unspoken was the knowledge that
by avoiding symbolic acts like that the men were
showing that there was enough inherent strength in
the movement to keep up the impetus without having to
generate that strength deliberately.

Yet on 28 September 1971, the co-ordinating
committee finally met in the boardroom. It was not so
much a sign of weakness as a realisation that the
forces they had feared all along were moving in on

them. They were under pressure to come to the
table and talk from both the official union side and the
Government. They met in the board room to show
that within the walls of the yards they could still do
as they decided.

The move was certainly not motivated by a desire
for better accommodation. The ventilation in the
boardroom in Linthouse was better than in the Clydebank classroom but the room had not been designed
for thirty to forty 'directors'.

Two days after the confrontation with Stenhouse
at the gates, a mass meeting of all the yards was
held in the Govan carpark. It was called to put the
'No co-operation' policy to the men. Till then each
division had met in separate mass meetings, but this
time the workforce were taken in a huge fleet of
buses to the one meeting.

The reason was obvious. There was pressure from
the press aimed at getting the Govan men to save
their jobs at the expense of the original 'four yards
together' policy.

At the time of the announcement of the advisory
committee's findings there had been universal shock
and outcry in Scotland. The Scottish press had
reflected this. The language, even of the right-wing
press, had been very similar to the stewards. As
Jimmy Reid recalled to the mass meeting, phrases
like 'carve up', 'disgusting', 'unacceptable' and
'butchery' had been used at the time.

Eight weeks before, Davies had been bashed for
saying he would only sanction one yard based on
Govan/Linthouse. Now he was trying to implement
that policy and he was being backed by many newspapers. Some, especially the Beaverbrook daily
and evening papers, openly supported the Government.
Others were less obvious but there had been a
perceptive difference in approach.

Time had been on the Government's side. Davies
knew that after several weeks of stalemate any change,
or at least the appearance of change, would seem to
be an improvement, and would be welcomed. He knew,
too, that anxiety was bound to build up - especially

since the unemployment figures were continually rising - and the straw of 2,500 jobs actually being proffered might break the wall of opposition.

The day after the announcement the Express ran an editorial article entitled: 'Clyde Killers! Is that what the unions want to be?' The Daily Record took a softer line. They appealed to 'Brother Dan' to 'speak up' and break the deadlock. A front page editorial acknowledged: 'The Record accepts that, after all the political pressure, Minister John Davies is trying to do something to save jobs on the Clyde'.

On the Friday morning the papers carried a stern statement from Davies reiterating that he would only put up money for Govan Shipbuilders if the unions entered talks about wages and conditions.

With all that pressure on the men the stewards were not going to risk the possibility of a Govan or Linthouse divisional meeting breaking away from the agreed line. (To be fair, I doubt if this would have happened). So the full 8,000 men were called together to give an overwhelming vote in favour of non co-operation.

As they were shouting 'Aye' at the top of their voices for the benefit of the T.V. cameras, 'Brother Dan' was speaking up in response to the Record's appeal. He told a reporter from the paper in his Newcastle office that he would be meeting Stenhouse next Wednesday, 29 September.

He said: 'Members elect leaders to lead them. And leaders don't have the privilege of taking dogmatic stands in a serious situation. When statements are made which leave no room for negotiations then that doesn't help the members'. He stressed that he saw a difference between preliminary talks with Stenhouse and formal negotiations on wages and conditions.

With pressure, then, from all sides, the co-ordinating committee decided to meet in the Linthouse boardroom on the 28th, to decide whether they should join McGarvey in the talks with Stenhouse.

The boardroom in the company's H.Q. is another room designed like a ship's cabin. This time, unlike the Clydebank classroom, the room is like the captain's suite on the QE2. It is decorated expensively with a large painted Maltese Cross - the company symbol - on the ceiling hiding the lighting. The symbol also appeared on the carpets.

The stewards sat or stood round the directors' table, with Airlie sitting in the chairman's seat. He was asked if the stewards had had difficulty getting into the boardroom. 'The flunkies are too scared to speak to the chairman of the board,' he joked. After the photographers had been allowed to record the scene for a few minutes, the door was closed and the 'Board Meeting: Please Do Not Disturb' sign was hung on the door.

A long discussion on the following day's talks took place with local officials of the unions. Eventually the men decided to meet with the 'Confed.' officials in the morning and in light of that meeting decide if they would send representatives to the meeting with Stenhouse. If they could get an assurance that the talks would cover all four yards 'cumulatively' they would come.

On Wednesday the unions met and McGarvey gave an assurance that the talks were to cover the future of all the yards. The two sides met in the North British Hotel in the city centre that afternoon. The talks went on for two and a half hours.

Halfway through them it became clear what kind of compromise might be reached. During an adjournment Stenhouse and Gilchrist emerged to announce that Ken Douglas had agreed to become the non-executive deputy Chairman of Govan Shipbuilders Ltd.

Three days before, Douglas had confirmed, on returning from holiday, that he had not been offered a position with the new company. He had repeatedly stated that he would not be willing to take a job which meant demotion or diminishment of power. So it seemed unlikely that, with the two top jobs taken, he would stay with shipbuilding on Clydeside.

On Monday afternoon, Gilchrist had lunch with Douglas to discuss the future of the yards. Nothing was said at the time, but on Tuesday Douglas dropped a broad hint that he might have some connection with the company on a 'freelance' basis.

He also went out of his way to emphasise his belief in the commercial future of Scotstoun yard. 'If someone would give me the assets and some working capital I could run Scotstoun yard at a profit,' he said. The facilities at Scotstoun and the capital equipment in use were no worse, he said, than they had been at Austin and Pickersgill and he had run that yard at a profit.

He went further than the Connells, who had said they would need Government finance and a tie-in with the Govan/Linthouse set-up to make the yard function profitably. Douglas was confident that while such a structure might be desirable it was not vital to the successful maintenance of Scotstoun.

When the appointment of Douglas was announced, it was no surprise to learn that Govan Shipbuilders had widened their scope to take an interest in the possibilities of Scotstoun. At the end of the talks it was stated that agreement had been reached that Scotstoun would be included in the feasibility study being made of Govan and Linthouse.

In return the unions recommended officially to the stewards a policy of co-operation. The stewards, said McGarvey, would consider making a 'gesture' when they next met.

The 'gesture' turned out to be inviting Stenhouse to visit the yards. Airlie formally invited the new chairman after Stenhouse had said that if he was given the full support of the workforce and Government capital for the project he would have no alternative but to give Clydebank serious consideration.

This was interpreted by the stewards as an acceptance of their basic policy that all four yards must be considered together. They took Stenhouse on a back-slapping - mainly by Stenhouse - tour of the yards. Once the tour was finished, however, Stenhouse went out of his way to stress that he had really meant that he would be interested only after agreement had been reached between the unions and the Government.

He told Ian Imrie of the Glasgow Herald: 'I think false hopes have been raised. I have never said I

127

The co-ordinating committee meet in the Linthouse boardroom

Stenhouse (l.) comes to agreement with McGarvie to begin meaningful talks. Next to Stenhouse are Gilchrist (seated) and Douglas (standing)

would take over Clydebank. This is beyond my resources.' Only if the two sides settled their differences and then money was available for Clydebank would he come into the picture.

Anyway by the beginning of October the situation began to look slightly healthier than it had on the date of liquidation or after publication of the report of the advisory committee. The U.C.S. situation had ceased to be primarily a political struggle and became once again a struggle based on industrial negotiations.

Till then, despite the presence of the liquidator, the confrontation had been directly between the workforce and the Government, with no referees between. At the beginning of the fight it had been assumed that the men would be engaged in a fight with Mr. Smith but he remained very much on the sidelines throughout. He passed on the commercial information to the Government who could either speed up or slow down the redundancies by manipulating the flow of cash to him or by giving, at a later stage, guarantees to firms with orders on the books.

The intervention of Stenhouse marked the end of the political struggle. No matter what show the co-ordinating committee put on it, the time for intransigence and total non co-operation was over. The purpose of these attitudes had been achieved. The Government had budged.

From October onwards the 'meaningful talks' moved forward cautiously. A large advance was made in getting the company going again as a trading proposition when the Government gave credit guarantees to the Irish Shipping Company and the Brazilian Government. These gave the green light for work to start on five more ships.

At this stage the future is still uncertain, unemployment is still rising and agreement on the thorny problems of wages and conditions has not been reached. The liquidator is still in charge at Linthouse and it will be many months, possibly a year, before a definitive forecast of the future of shipbuilding on the upper reaches of the Clyde.

The short term future looks brighter than it has for

many months but the long-term economic decline
of the heavy traditional industries in the west of
Scotland remains a hard fact. With unemployment
reaching its peak in the winter months of 1971 the
Government cannot long ignore its responsibility for
halting that trend or at least providing an alternative
- honourable work.

But the pressure for that wider achievement will
be led now by the co-ordinating bodies like the
T.U.C. and S.T.U.C. They now have the movement,
the solidarity and the impetus created by the fight
of the 8,500 men of Upper Clyde Shipbuilders. And
they have the slogan on which to base that pressure -
the U.C.S. stewards' demand for 'The Right to Work'.

XIII

WHO WAS TO BLAME?

The Battle of Upper Clyde Shipbuilders was fought over the mortally wounded body of the company, with both sides arguing that the other had been responsible for striking the blow.

That the workers were to blame was only to be expected from a Conservative Government. Yet it was put across rather lamely and, in the case of some of the principal Tories involved, not at all.

When Benn had been Minister of Technology in the summer of 1969, he had demanded a revamping of the management coupled with a run down of the labour force. As his reasons for this demand, he had given the need for reduced absenteeism, fewer unofficial stoppages, better management and higher productivity.

When liquidation happened it was rather difficult to point at these same failings as a contribution to the system. Strikes, especially over demarcation had dropped; absenteeism had fallen from the 1969 figure of 9 per cent to the national average, through sickness, of 5 per cent. While Ridley had not been impressed by the U.C.S. management, there were few experts in the industry unwilling to give praise to Douglas.

It would not be an exaggeration to say that relations between the workforce and the management had never been better in the history of Clydeside shipbuilding. New productivity techniques were being introduced and the men were beginning to co-operate. This very success of industrial relations and productivity in the company flashes a danger sign for future attempts to create the same or better management-worker relations in shipbuilding.

Jimmy Reid has often pointed out in speeches: 'How can you go and argue with the British workers that the solution to the economic problems of Britain are 'That You Shall Increase Production' when they can turn round and say, 'You told that to the U.C.S. workers, they responded, and you put the boot in and butchered them?'

James Ramsay, the Clyde district full-time official of the Boilermakers' Society has similar forebodings. 'We gave them (U.C.S.) inter-changeability, flexibility, mobility. We sat on production committees that, at one time, trade unionists would never have agreed to sit on.

'It rings a warning to you. Because if this is gonna be the Government's attitude then there's not gonna be any co-operation from the working class.' It took years of hard work by forward-looking ship-builders like Douglas and Ken Alexander and intelligent trade unionists like the late William Hutchison to coax the men and some unions from entrenched distrust of productivity and flexibility methods in the shipyards.

The U.C.S. demise could easily send them back to the days of insular solidarity defended by demarcation lines.

If it was not too easy to blame the workers then the Government had a bloody good try at blaming the company management. John Davies is an accountant and naturally sees success or failure in these terms. That the company was launching a ship every three and a half weeks did not matter if the figures did not look good.

And of course they never had. The company had always been short of working capital, always been on the razor's edge of an excess of liabilities. The various rescue operations of further capital injections had always been 'too little, too late'. There are few shipbuilding companies in Britain who do not know the situation.

It was Davies' contention that he knew nothing of the seriousness of the situation till 9 June 1971. The

company had failed, he said, to keep himself and the
S.I.B. informed. He repeatedly inferred in the
Commons debate on 15 June that the management had
either ignored the problem or had hidden it.

I shall deal in a moment with the causes of the
company's difficulties in summer 1971, but, accepting
they existed, did the company make no attempt to
inform the Government?

On 3 May 1971, Davies received a letter from the
company containing much detailed analysis of the
financial situation. It enclosed the accounts for the
first quarter of 1971, a statement of the projected
trading results to December 1971, a statement of
projected and actual results for September 1970 to
9 April 1971, and a long-term forecast of the company's
performance.

When the existence of this letter was raised,
Davies agreed he had received it and added: 'Bless my
soul, it gave no indication whatever of such a serious
situation as I was faced with on Wednesday of last
week'. (Official Report, 15 June 1971; vol. 819, c.239)

In fact the letter stated explicitly: 'While the
trading results are showing a most encouraging trend,
the cash position continues to be acutely difficult'. If
that was not explicit enough the letter also pointed out
that the figures had been revised to 'take account of
the disruption caused to our shipbuilding programme
due to the acute and increasing shortage of funds at
that time.' A reference to the heavy creditor pressure
during the period when the credits had been stopped
only a few months before.

As another indication of the cash problems the
letter requested that the interest on the loans given
in 1968 and 1969 be written off by the Government.
Davies was also aware that the company were anxious
to complete a capital re-construction involving the
writing down of most if not all of the £21 million
given or loaned at one time or another by the Labour
Government.

Davies has also confirmed that the company
regularly provided monthly management accounts,
cash flow forecasts, profit projections and weekly

production statistics to him. So he can have been in little doubt that the company was still on that razor's edge.

Professor Alexander is one who rejects the assessment made by Davies of the company's accounting: 'The general financial management of the company was good. Shipbuilding is, after all, difficult to manage financially, particularly in an inflationary situation.

'It is not very easy when you are making a one-off product over a two-year production cycle with wages rising at 10 per cent per annum and the process involves assembling hundreds of various components into a final product.

'Most manufacturing is very much easier over a shorter period, with a shorter production cycle.'

In any case, as Alexander points out, if the Government felt that it was not getting adequate information they were, as the biggest shareholder, in an excellent position to demand it.

He told me: 'I think it should be said that any day the Government or the S.I.B. wanted information about the current financial situation at Upper Clyde they could have phoned up and they would have got the most up-to-date information available.

'The company was really in the Government's pocket and I don't know what delayed them.'

The only experience Davies had of engineering before going into the cabinet was a short spell as a director of Black and Decker where the product, and the style of production and assembly, was worlds apart from shipbuilding.

The other major criticism of the management was made by the 'Four Wise Men' who claimed that the order book had been too thin.

At the time of liquidation the order book had thirty ships commissioned worth over £90 million. At the same time, the order book for the whole British shipbuilding industry was for 312 ships worth £690 million so the U.C.S. orders were worth 13 per cent of the total value of the British order book.

The U.C.S. board justified the order book's

condition by claiming that it only included orders
for two years ahead as a deliberate policy. It was
felt that with inflation rising all the time it would
be dangerous to fix the price of a ship three or
four years before you bought the materials to build
it.

Ken Douglas said: 'When people talk about the order
book being thin, this is part of a deliberate policy,
recognised by anyone who knows the business.

'On fixed prices to plan three, four or five years
ahead is just madness. I deliberately keep a two
years' order book so you can reasonably calculate
your forward prices and when there is a suitable
market, you have early berths to offer and early
deliveries. '

Alexander agreed: 'Given the pace of inflation it
was quite a sensible policy. That was assuming you
were going to be continuously in business over the
period. '

The company was not, of course, in business over
the period. The four-month moratorium on credit
between October 1970 and February 1971 meant that
the company had not been able to take any orders. So
any hope of continuity by quick turnover and a
short-term order book was broken.

In any case, the company were in an advanced stage
of negotiations on orders worth £100 million consisting
of twenty product carriers worth £5 million each.
When the stewards claimed that these orders had
been in the grasp of U.C.S. and had been killed by
liquidation the D.O.T.I. vigorously denied their
existence.

But no less an authority than Ken Douglas had been
relying on these orders to save the company from
liquidation. The day before the liquidator was
appointed, he told Stewart Fraser of the Glasgow
Herald: 'If U.C.S. can stay in business, they are in
line to win orders worth at least £100 million -
enough to keep them going to the end of 1974...nobody
can offer as early delivery dates. '

The company had adopted a parallel policy to the
short-term order book to try and combat the tight

grip inflation had on their finances. They had been able to negotiate, probably for the first time in British shipbuilding, an agreement with the steel suppliers that payments for steel would be made on a fixed-price basis.

Unfortunately, the system never had time to prove itself for when liquidation left the B.S.C. with heavy losses they naturally insisted on raising the price of steel supplied to the liquidator in an attempt to recoup some of their loss.

Blamed equally by Davies and the advisory committee was Anthony Wedgwood Benn, though the criticism was usually undefined and in the form of phrases like 'mistakes in creation'.

Much of the sting has been taken out of these attacks by Benn's own admission that he now feels he made a mistake in not bringing the whole shipbuilding industry under public ownership back in 1968. Since then most yards now have substantial Government shareholding involvement and with the exception of Austin and Pickersgill and Scott-Lithgow the major yards in Britain are controlled by the state, if not in name, certainly in reality.

Benn too failed to take heed of the Geddes provision for a 'fresh start' for the industry that required a new kind of management and organisation as well as 'new money and some new men'.

It was not till August 1969 that Benn realised that by placing so many of the old guard of Clydeside shipbuilding on the new U.C.S. board, he had blocked the way to the 'fresh start'. Douglas was the kind of new man that Geddes was talking about, but he was given too little time and, of course, too little money, to speedily reverse the cumbersome procedure of the yards.

Nobody would deny that the company's shortage of money in 1969 coincided with the peak of the Labour Government's fiscal problems, but it might have been wiser in the long term to have complied just once with the company's estimate of its needs.

If the mortal wounding had not been at the hands of the workers, and the management were equally unwilling to accept blame, who did they accuse?

The Government were blamed loud and long by the U.C.S. stewards. Douglas too had some hard words to say about them. Even Anthony Hepper, who had quietly left the chairman's office on the arrival of the liquidator and has been silent on the subject since, let it be known that he had felt since November 1970 that the Government was preparing to disengage from the company.

There is no lack of evidence to point to the intent of the Conservative Government to kill off 'lame ducks' like U.C.S. And there was little sign of regret by the cheering backbenchers, especially the Scottish Tories, who greeted the announcement of liquidation with glee.

Whether the Government deliberately brought about the collapse is more difficult to assess.

They stopped the credits in October 1970 without telling the company they were going to. There was little sign of willingness to restore them till the company was teetering on the edge again in February when, in the same week as the Rolls Royce collapse, they were suddenly restored.

The Government did agree to a capital reconstruction in January 1971 when the owners agreed to pay the company 5 per cent more for their ships. Yet the reconstruction had still not been effected over four months later when liquidation happened. In all that time there was no sign of the D.O.T.I. expressing any interest in the progress of the reconstruction proposals.

The only reconstruction that made any sense was a writing down of much, if not all, of the money owed to the Government. As John Davies said, the money was irretrievably sunk in the company, so why not write it off and give the company a fresh start?

Neither the reconstruction nor the increased payments by the owners were able to come to the company's rescue. By June, many of the ships were still being built and U.C.S. had not received much of the extra 5 per cent.

But if the Government were trying to kill off U.C.S.

by neglect, why did they restore the credits in February? There are two possible reasons - apart from the claim by Davies and Ridley that they had new hope for the company as a result of the promise of a reconstruction. One is that the crisis caused by the withdrawal of credits came to a head too near the Rolls Royce crash. The other is that Yarrow's had to be hived off before the company could be allowed to collapse.

The treatment given to Yarrow's was in complete contrast to that given to U.C.S. The former yard got a lavish £4½ million loan to see it through future difficulties. It also had the only modern development created in the short history of U.C.S. - the covered berth. But the Government had strong reasons for supporting the continuance of Yarrow's. There is, after all, little point in having a policy of selling frigates to South Africa if you kill off the only yard which can build them.

The solution of liquidation adopted by the Government can now be seen to be a political choice. There is no logic in terms of profit and loss - a credo beloved of Conservatives - for throwing so many people out of work. There is now much evidence that the cost of making 6,000 men redundant would have been far greater than giving the £6 million working capital asked for in June 1971.

Equally it is clear that the company would have been moving into profitability by 1972. The Government was already in receipt of the S.I.B. annual report when it decided in favour of liquidation. The report for the year ended 31 March 1971 contained a forecast of a happier future. It was sent to the D.O.T.I. on 15 May, a full month before the liquidator took over.

It stated: 'There were signs of improvement at the beginning of 1971. Old and troublesome contracts had been completed, the labour force had been brought into line with future requirements, settlements had been reached with the unions, and the company's order book was such that new orders for early delivery could be taken on satisfactory terms. '

It also noted that with the help from shipowners, the

138

end of loss-making contracts, more stable industrial relations and improved production, the company 'should make the long awaited turn to profitability'.

This report must have been seen by John Davies.

Douglas, Alexander and others more closely involved with the company have repeatedly stressed that they were confident the company was indeed about to lose its loss-making tag.

In terms of cost, too, there was little sense in killing off Upper Clyde. By November 1971, just over 1,000 men had been paid off by the liquidator. A survey by the Daily Record has estimated that by early 1972 the Government would have had to fork out £35 million.

The liquidator had spent £14 million on wages and materials. The Government has promised £5 million to cover losses on future ships for the Irish Shipping Company. (Despite boasts by Ridley that the money given in June to the liquidator to keep the company going would be repaid by the profits from these ships.)

The S.T.U.C. has calculated that the average redundancy pay is £300, so for the first 1,000 Upper Clyde men paid off the Government has paid out £300,000. On Clydeside it took six months on average to find a new job for a shipbuilding worker - in autumn 1971 there were thirty-five men chasing each available job in Glasgow - at a cost of six months' social security money for each family.

It was clear that few of these men would find other jobs in shipbuilding, so new jobs had to be found. Government figures show that in 1971 it costs about £1,500 per new job brought to Scotland. There is also the loss of each man's taxes as well as his rates and rents which have to be met by a Government-financed rebate. Like it or not, the taxpayers of south-east England had to pay out much more to the unemployed of Upper Clyde than they had the right to expect from the Government they elected.

The money paid out for the 1,000 redundant men alone could easily be over the £6 million asked for by the company. The cost of paying off 6,000 men along with over 10,000 in ancillary industries would be astronomical.

It's an expensive way to find out that it is cheaper to nurse the lame duck back to health than to shoot it.

XIV

'MORE THAN THE RIGHT TO BE EMPLOYED'

It is customary, when receiving an award in show business circles, to make a modest speech saying it was all really the work of others - the producer, the director, the boys in the backroom. Jimmy Reid, as the 'Most Promising Political Newcomer of 1971', would be the first to give credit to both his colleagues, and the movement they led, for his sudden rise to national importance.

He began the year as a shipbuilding engineer, a member of a much distrusted political party and a town councillor in a small Scottish burgh. He ended it as the subject of several T.V. programmes and newspaper articles. The Late Night Line Up programme on B.B.C.2 flew up to Glasgow to devote a whole programme to him. Jimmy Young brought his morning radio show to Clydebank, 'because it's in the news' and introduced the whole Reid family to his M.M.M.M.F.* Reid was offered a record programme on Radio 4 to himself by the Scottish B.B.C.

To say that the boys in the classroom were the whole reason for this interest would be unfair to Reid's own considerable personality. But there can be no doubt that the massive interest of the media was an achievement of the campaign. There were other, more vital, aims and in these too the stewards were successful.

---

*'Many Millions of Mid-Morning Friends' - over five million, in fact.

Yarrow yard showing (top l.) the covered berth, and a South African frigate being fitted out

James Reid

The most basic test of success for the 'work-in' must be 'did it save jobs?' It certainly kept men in employment for several months after they had been handed their cards by the liquidator.

By November, just over 1,000 workers were no longer employed by the company. About 200 left through retirement. Another 400 either left at once when receiving their notice or found other work after 'working-in' for a month or two. The rest, over 400, stayed on and handed their cards to the co-ordinating committee.

Clydebank naturally had the highest stay-on rate - there was least alternative employment there. Scotstoun too had a high percentage. Convener Sam Barr claims that the local yard management contributed to this by nominating the best-known radicals for redundancy. Certainly within a few weeks of the lay-offs beginning, he was the only leading steward in the yard still on the payroll.

The great fear at the beginning was that the incentive of redundancy payments, being offered to men volunteering for redundancy, would prove too strong an attraction to hold the solidarity. Once a man had been laid off at the choice of the liquidator there was no difficulty. He could take the redundancy money and stay on.

But the stewards took the attitude that anyone who wrote to the liquidator offering to become redundant had sold out the principles of the 'work-in' and could not stay. So if anyone accepted the carrot of redundancy money, they were opting out of the work force completely. The liquidator supplied the stewards with the names of those who had volunteered once he had laid them off. He had been unwilling to do so, but the unions pointed out that they were paying out dispute money to those 'working-in' and they wanted to be certain the individual was in dispute.

It must be counted as a victory for the stewards, and the militancy they created in the yards, that of 8,500 workers only 350 to 400 men took the carrot in the three months of 'working-in'.

There was also, of course, in the mind of every

man considering his future, the knowledge that
unemployment was rising continually as winter
approached and with each month there were more and
more men chasing fewer and fewer jobs.

In relation to the excitement and interest the whole
affair generated, it might seem that the actual numbers
directly making a stand and 'working-in' are small.
It should be noted that as well as saving the above
number from the dole there is little doubt that the
campaign prevented many more redundancies.

The liquidator announced, after the advisory
committee report was issued, that he intended to
deplete the labour force by 1,400 men by the beginning
of October. By that time only half that number had
been paid off. Mr. Smith always stressed that he
was an officer of the court and his decisions had to
be based on purely economic grounds, with the
interests of the creditors coming first.

The halving of the redundancy programme therefore
can only have been accomplished because the
Government was willing to put up extra money to keep
more men in work. So the Government was paying
the men's wages rather than have them become a
liability to the stewards' Fighting Fund!

It was often said by critics that the 'work-in' was
a publicity measure, involving no real control of the
yards. The New Statesman described the takeover and
'work-in' as 'an effective piece of theatre'.

In a sense this is true. There was no intent to
create a workers' commune in the yards. Airlie
summed up the stewards' attitude in answer to a
young Scandinavian journalist who asked, 'Is this a
new form of industrial revolution?'. He replied:
'Our only purpose is to save the jobs of the men. If,
as a by product, a new form of protest or control
comes about then that is welcome - but it is not our
aim.'

Nonetheless there were isolated occasions when
the men asserted their control in a more meaningful
way than merely checking the traffic going in and out
of the gates.

Ship 121 is a good example. The ship's future was

uncertain during the first weeks of the 'work-in'. The liquidator was unwilling to start work on a boat without any guarantee it would be completed. There was also the fear that if he did order a start it would be at Govan rather than, as originally planned, at Scotstoun.

The basic structure was already in fifty-ton units at Linthouse and the stewards planned to take it over by barge - with the co-operation of the tugboatmen's union - and start work on the keel at Scotstoun.

It was learned that the liquidator planned to sell the large crane at Linthouse which was necessary to load the heavy steel units onto the barge. The liquidator was told bluntly it was not to be sold and it wasn't. He was also told that if he did not move the units to Scotstoun the men would.

The liquidator took the hint and ordered over the keel. That incident too kept more jobs on Mr. Smith's payroll than would have been expected.

There were other examples. Drawing boards were sold from the planning office in Govan, but were not allowed to leave the yard. After laying off many painters in Clydebank at the beginning of August, Mr. Smith found he needed some again in November. He informed the stewards he intended to recruit painters from the labour exchange. He was told there were six painters in the yard 'working-in' and they could be employed. He took them and didn't look for any more from outside. The same happened later with electricians.

But these are lesser achievements than the overall success of the campaign. There is no question that the men reversed the course of Government policy. They put what seemed a shameless Government to shame. In the summer of 1970, the Tories came to power promising to deal firmly with the 'lame ducks' and if men lost their jobs, the market pressures would find them others. By the winter of 1971 they were pumping hundreds of millions of pounds into the economy in a belated attempt to prevent unemployment topping the million mark for the first time since the thirties.

By the imaginative action of the men of Upper Clyde, a focal point was created for the widespread opposition to the Government's policies. They attracted support from every section of the organised working class as well as from many 'liberal' institutions like the Church and the universities.

Bodies like the Confederation of Shipbuilding and Engineering Unions, the British and Scottish Trades Union Congresses and the Labour Party like to feel they meet together annually to discuss national issues and decide on the wider aspects of unemployment. Yet they all went out of their way at their annual meetings to identify in the fullest possible way with the struggle of the workers of one company among thousands having to cope with redundancy.

The Upper Clyde catalyst was at work when the T.U.C. adopted as its theme for a campaign on unemployment the phrase 'The Right to Work'. The catalyst was at work when the workers of Plessey occupied their factory in Alexandria and refused to allow the capital equipment to be taken south to Ilford.

It was at work when the steel workers in Sheffield decided to fight the threat to 4,000 jobs in the massive B.S.C. plant at River Don. They wrote defiantly on the factory wall, 'B.S.C. is yours - we will fight to keep it'.

In a sense it was at work when hundreds of ordinary councillors in British local authorities decided that they too were unwilling to accept unjust policies or laws. They openly flaunted or broke the Education (Milk) Act and ordered free milk to be given to school-children in hundreds of primary schools.

In a long-term assessment of the significance of the events of 1971 on the upper reaches of the Clyde, the spin off from the men's action is still happening and will continue for a long time. 'The Right to Work' is now recognised as a basic human right and who can doubt that fighting to defend that right is correct.

But the fight was more than just a defence of a right to be employed. In Scotland it involved something

146

more. It was a last effort to assert that with the advance of technology and automation there must be no loss of dignity in men's employment.

The men of Upper Clyde feel pride in their work. They wanted to maintain that pride, to show that they could create as well as manufacture. They wanted to build ships.

In ten years' time can a heavy-built ex-boilermaker be expected to look at the 396th perfect micro-circuit he has turned out in a morning and still feel the same emotions he feels when he sees a ship hit the water at the foot of the slipway, when he smelt the rusty dust of the drag chains?

Can he be expected to look at that micro-circuit and feel pride that it's 'Clyde Built'?

As long as ships have to be built, it's vital to the Clydeside psyche that we build them. When they stop shipbuilding here, we will all lose something within ourselves - forever.

HOUSE OF COMMONS
LONDON, S.W.1

<u>PRIVATE AND CONFIDENTIAL</u>

<u>NOTE OF A MEETING BETWEEN NICHOLAS
RIDLEY AND SIR ERIC YARROW OF
YARROW (SHIPBUILDERS) - part of U.C.S. -
3rd December, 1969.</u>

1. U.C.S. owes £7 million now, and would need perhaps £12 million more public money to get it afloat safely. Its immediate liquidity crisis appears to have been temporarily solved by the S.I.B. paying the weekly wages - but a decision by the Government as to the future is urgent. He expects them to provide funds to last only until the next election!

2. U.C.S. wages are 20 per cent higher than Lower Clyde. Lower Clyde men are on strike to achieve parity. A decision to save U.C.S. would have very serious repercussions indeed upon Lower Clyde, with £100 million order book.

3. Yarrow's has suffered grievously through the merger, both in profits, and in labour relations. They are being dragged down by this vast, loss-making and badly-run concern.

4. The best long term solution is, having regard to the politics of the situation as well as the economics:-

   a. Detach Yarrow from U.C.S. and allow it to be independent prior to merging on agreed terms with Lower Clyde, or Thorneycroft.

   b. For the Government (Labour or Tory) to bail out the rest of U.C.S. - to write off its debts, sell off Government shareholdings, close one or even two of its three yards, appoint a new chairman, and let it stand or fall on its own.

This might cost £10 million, but would be the end of the nightmare.

c. To work toward an eventual merger of Lower Clyde, Yarrow, U.C.S.

d. The employment effects of this would be small. Perhaps thus:- (very approximately)

	NOW	AFTER
U.C.S.)	13,000	5,000
Yarrow)		6,000
Lower Clyde		+1,000 extra.
	13,000	12,000

5. The alternative is the continuance of huge losses, or the collapse of U.C.S. and 13,000 unemployed.

6. I believe we should work out the scheme in (4.) above in more detail, get it agreed with all concerned, and then make it our policy.

c.c. The Rt. Hon. Sir Keith Joseph, Bt., M.P.
Miss Betty Harvie Anderson, O.B.E., M.P.
Gordon Campbell, Esq., M.C., M.P.

FROM: NICHOLAS RIDLEY, M.P.

HOUSE OF COMMONS
U.C.S. Ltd.   LONDON, S.W.1

CONFIDENTIAL

Saw A. Hepper and K. Douglas of U.C.S. and I also
spent morning with Lower Clyde Directors.

U.C.S. comprises five Companies - Yarrow, Fair-
Fields, Stephens, John Brown, and Connells.

'Rationalization' so far has meant the closing of one
yard - Stephens. Production has been concentrated as
follows:-

Yarrow	Naval ships	
Govan	(Fairfields)	Bulk Carriers
Clydebank	(John Browns)	Big ships (not Tankers)
Scotstoun	(Connell's)	General Cargo ships Cargo Liners (Standard 'Clyde' Merchant ships)

There are no plans to close further yards. (These
concentrations of ship types could in fact have been
carried out without amalgamation)

There has been little centralization of facilities -
only joinery shops and computers, so far; and only
little more planned.

Other advantages claimed for the grouping of the five
yards are a common labour policy, and the ability to
take larger orders. The advantages appear to be
surprisingly small.

U.C.S. is limited by the size of the river to 100,000
tonnage.

U.C.S. has had £20.2 million of public money - $\frac{3}{4}$'s in loans, $\frac{1}{4}$ in grants. See Appendix 1.

It inherited huge losses from the constituent companies - particularly Fairfields and John Browns. (These should have remained the responsibility of the Companies and not been made U.C.S.'s responsibility. This was done on the Tyne.

Orders are now considerable. There is doubt as to whether:

        (a) they are enough.
        (b) they are profitable enough.

There seems to be good prospects for the new Standard 19000 Ton 'Clyde' merchant ship. U.C.S. is, naturally, more confident about the future than anyone else.

Hepper and Douglas assured me that the £7 million now proposed would be the last injection of public money needed. It is not generally thought that this is true, and the estimate is that more will be needed at the end of the year - perhaps another £5 million.

Annual turnover is about £35 million in merchant ships
                      £15 million in naval ships.

No major capital expenditure is planned and only £1 million is to be spent on minor improvements in the near future.

U.C.S. employs 10,500 men, reducing to 7,500 by the middle of 1970, as contracts are completed.

Management claim a 20 per cent increase in labour productivity over the past 4 months. (Due to a productivity bonus scheme.) This only brings it up to average levels for shipbuilding.

Wages are up to £30 a week take home pay, which is 20 per cent above Lower Clyde. It is similar to the wage levels paid on Wear and Tyne.
No security of employment or bargain with the men. Labour relations appear less advanced than in many other yards.

Morale is bad. U.C.S. is described by Lower Clyde as a 'Cancer' eating into the whole of Clydeside Industrial Life. Firms are being encouraged by the Unions to go bust so that the state will take over responsibility for paying higher wages. Pressure on these lines had been applied even at Rolls Royce. Huge wage demands are being backed with this suggestion quite openly.

Top Management consists of three only - Hepper, Douglas and Crawford (Finance). I am not impressed by them. There is little devolution.

The Government's Guarantee of performance which Benn mentioned in his statement in December '69, is in order to match Japanese offers. The Japs are offering to guarantee delivery, and Owners are demanding similar offers from U.K. yards. It is quite wrong to restrict guarantees to U.C.S. alone. It is probably wrong for the Government to give them at all. U.C.S. policy is to resist giving guarantees, and they have been forced to give one by one owner only, though more may be required in future. They do not yet constitute a major financial liability, therefore.

Relations with Yarrow's are extremely strained. Eric Yarrow is publicly attacking U.C.S., and doing everything he can to extract Yarrow's from U.C.S. There is no reason why Yarrow's should not leave U.C.S., except (according to U.C.S.) that it would 'leave Yarrow's in an exposed and dangerous situation'. Eric Yarrow wrote a critical article in the Shipbuilding and Shipping Industry Record of December 19th and 20th, 1939.

CONCLUSION

I believe that we should do the following on assuming office:-

(a) Give no more public money to U.C.S.
(b) Let Yarrow's leave U.C.S. if they still want to, and facilitate their joining Lower Clyde if they

153

still wish to do so.

(c) This would lead to the bankruptcy of U.C.S.

We could accept this, in which case Lower Clyde would take over one or two of the yards. The employment result would be:

	1970	Then	(Men)
Yarrow's		4,000	
U.C.S.	7,500		
Lower Clyde	7,000	9,000	
	14,500	13,000	

i.e. 1500 men would be redeployed to other works and would be rapidly reemployed.

We could put in a Government 'Butcher' to cut up U.C.S. and to sell (cheaply) to Lower Clyde, and others, the assets of U.C.S., to minimise upheaval and dislocation. I am having further views on the practicality of such an operation, which I will report.

(d) After liquidation or reconstruction as above, we should sell the Government holding in U.C.S., even for a pittance.

At this stage we should confine ourselves to saying absolutely firmly that there will be no more money from the Tory Government. Hepper and Douglas say they do not need any more; so such a statement will not put us into conflict either with U.C.S., or with Benn.

When we get in, we are clear to take either of the courses set out in 21 (c) above. If U.C.S. becomes viable we merely adopt 21 (d).

We should hammer the point that this chaos is the result of the appalling blunder of George Brown's intervention to save Fairfields. It is a prime example of the folly of Government Intervention.

154

REPORT OF THE ADVISORY GROUP ON SHIPBUILDING ON THE UPPER CLYDE

Upper Clyde Shipbuilders

1. The causes and circumstances of the failure of U.C.S., which contrasts sadly with the performance of other shipbuilding enterprises on the Clyde can be summarised as follows:-

(a) a totally mistaken initial structure which forced together into one rigid and prestigious Group five companies whose shipbuilding competitiveness was exceedingly doubtful unless major improvements in facilities and methods were brought about urgently and whose financial strength was fragile. This imposed annual Group expenses of something over £2 million net of loan interest:

(b) a massive drain from an already weak Working Capital by the absorption in U.C.S. of losses from pre-existing contracts which in August 1968 had been estimated at £3.55 million but which, in fact, have totalled over £12 million:

(c) a mistaken marketing policy which led to losses on new contracts which already in August 1968 were known to amount to £4.8 million but which, in fact, have totalled £9.8 million:

(d) in the result, the total injection of public funds has disappeared. No improvement in facilities, no worthwhile investment has been made. Facilities remain as they were before the merger, ill-equipped and cramped at Clydebank, less out-of-date but still more cramped at Scotstoun, and even at Govan by no means modern although much better in available space so vital for modern shipbuilding:

(e) the mistake in original structure and the subsequent happenings were compounded by poor management, for the continuation of which until

155

June 1971 Government and the Shipbuilding Industry Board must bear their share of responsibility:

(f) in particular, management has not exercised efficient control of costs, particularly of wages, which in their impact seriously threatened other industry on the Clyde:

(g) it is true that recently there is evidence of improvement in productivity which we recognise has made events even more of a shock to men when from a production viewpoint they thought they were rounding a corner. But this improvement does not offset the inherent weaknesses in the present structure and facilities of U.C.S.

2. CONCLUSION

2.1 The conclusion must be that any continuation of Upper Clyde Shipbuilders in its present form would be wholly unjustified and, indeed, could cause serious and more widespread damage. It is important that the lessons of this failure are clear and unambiguous.

3. RECOMMENDATIONS

3.1 In these Recommendations we have tried to make judgments primarily on grounds of likely commercial viability both in a short and longer term sense, but, in view of Government's share of responsibility, we have also given weight to social considerations which we believe Government in this case must observe. Our Recommendations, subject to the approval as appropriate of the Liquidator, are as follows:-

(1) that an end be made to U.C.S. whilst retaining legal and financial flexibility to help achieve other objectives:

(2) that a successor company is established at Govan/Linthouse, and that Clydebank and Scotstoun be disposed of as soon as possible by the Liquidator:

(3) that the present shipbuilding programme is concentrated so far as is practicable, and as urgently as possible, upon the Govan yard. In achieving this, we would note that individual contracts may be re-negotiated wherever there is potential benefit. We should also mention that there is considerable misunderstanding about this present programme. Looked at in total it may seem large but spread as it was over the three U.C.S. yards it was already dangerously thin in the light of the present depressed conditions in world shipping. If this programme can be concentrated partly or largely into Govan/Linthouse, however, a more valuable base order book would be achieved:

(4) that every assistance is given by Government and the Local Authorities in assisting re-deployment of redundant staff and workers, particularly in the shipyards on the Lower Clyde at Yarrow's and elsewhere. It is our understanding that Scott-Lithgow could immediately absorb 1,000 men and that Yarrow's in certain circumstances might be able to absorb a number of steel workers. Furthermore the completion of existing new buildings in the three U.C.S. yards and the transfer to Govan of other new buildings where keels have not yet been laid will all take a little time which could be valuable in phasing out redundancies so that natural retirements due to age etc. have the greatest possible influence.

3.2 It is our believe that shipbuilding can be undertaken with good prospects of profitability at Govan. The yard is suitable for building bulkcarriers up to around 70,000 tons deadweight and should be well placed to compete efficiently in this range of size, which includes ships such as product-carriers. We would not recommend any extension above the upper limit until at least five years of viable performance had been recorded.

157

3.3 On the basis of present facilities, we believe that six ships of some 30,000 tons deadweight could be completed each year involving a steel output of some 30,000 or 40,000 tons. Efficient production on this scale would probably give stable employment in the first stage for some 2,000 men and 500 staff. In securing longer term viability, improvement in productivity should be capable of being achieved up to some 50 per cent above present levels.

3.4 An essential contribution towards this would be a commitment by the Unions to accept certain changes in working practices including in due course a change to a 2-shift daily working, say from 6 a.m. to 2 p.m. and from 2 p.m. to 10 p.m., with night working limited to maintenance. By such means, an increase in output to eight ships of the type mentioned might be possible, which in turn could justify an investment programme of perhaps £1.5 million in improving cranes and lifting facilities within Govan and perhaps, on a larger scale later, of extension of facilities in Linthouse.

3.5 We must emphasise that these recommendations in respect of the continuation of shipbuilding at Govan are conditional on: -

(1) the full co-operation of the Unions in making this venture succeed and, in particular, in the acceptance of shift working of the type suggested above, together with competitive wage rates:

(2) adequate capital being forthcoming:

(3) satisfactory management.

3.6 Union participation both on a national and local basis has to be secured and this might be done in a Working Party set up to establish this new company. In the terms of reference for such a Working Party there must be no doubt at all that the proposal represents the one and only effective alternative to a total cessation of shipbuilding on the Upper Clyde. It should be stated however, that this is an alternative which, in our commercial judgment, we believe should be viable and capable also of expansion in the years to come.

3.7 We recognise that the financial support needed to establish the new company will not be easy to obtain. A degree of Government involvement will be necessary in any event if the support of suppliers of marine equipment and other goods and services on the one hand and of shipowners on the other is to be obtained. Initially the Government may have to bear the total financial burden, either by making resources available or by the provision of guarantees or by a combination of both.

3.8 The success or failure of this venture will depend fundamentally on management. It is rarely possible to produce a satisfactory management structure at the drop of a hat. Efficient operation of the unit on a day-to-day basis must be secured; executive responsibility must be precise and unblurred. It has been suggested that this could be achieved under the overall policy direction of a Temporary Management Committee, to be set up immediately and to include representatives of others engaged in the shipbuilding industry in Britain. Such representatives would have to be chosen very carefully to ensure that this is not just a paper solution but is a body capable of taking action and monitoring action. On these conditions such an arrangement could bridge the initial period and lead the way to the adoption of a final management structure a little later.

We are not able to commit ourselves finally at this stage to this suggestion, but we believe it worthy of consideration as part of the essential steps to establish a new shipbuilding company at Govan.

GLOSSARY OF ABBREVIATIONS

A.E.U.	:-	The Amalgamated Engineering Union (now part of A.U.E.W.)
A.U.E.W.	:-	Amalgamated Union of Engineering Workers
B.S.C.	:-	British Steel Corporation
'Buroo'	:-	The Labour Exchange
C.B.I.	:-	Confederation of British Industry
C.D.A.	:-	Clydeside Development Authority
'Confed.'	:-	The Confederation of Shipbuilding and Engineering Unions
D.C.L.	:-	Distillers Company Ltd.
D.O.T.I.	:-	Department of Trade and Industry
G.M.W.U.	:-	General and Municipal Workers' Union
I.R.A.	:-	Industrial Relations Act
'Lower Clyde'	:-	The Scott-Lithgow group of shipyards
S.I.B.	:-	Shipbuilding Industry Board
S.I.H.	:-	Shipping Industrial Holdings Ltd.
S.N.P.	:-	Scottish National Party
S.T.U.C.	:-	Scottish Trades Union Congress
T.U.C.	:-	Trades Union Congress
U.C.S.	:-	Upper Clyde Shipbuilders Ltd.